THE
LINERS

THE LINERS

ROB MCAULEY

CONSULTANT:
WILLIAM H. MILLER

Motorbooks International

This edition first published in 1997 by Motorbooks International Publishers &
Wholesalers, 729 Prospect Avenue, PO Box 1, Osceola, WI 54020 USA.

© (text) The Liners Pty. Ltd. 1997.

Previously published by Boxtree, an imprint of Macmillan Publishers Ltd.,
25 Eccleston Place, London, SW1W 9NF and Basingstoke..

Motorbooks International is a certified trademark, registered with the United
States Patent Office.

The information in this book is true and complete to the best of our
knowledge. All recommendations are made without any guarantee on the part
of the author or publisher, who also disclaim any liability incurred in connection with the
use of this data or specific details.

We recognize that some words, model names and designations, for example,
mentioned herein are the property of the trademark holder. We use them for
identification purposes only. This is not an official publication.

Motorbooks International books are also available at discounts in bulk quantity
for industrial or sales-promotional use. For details write to special sales
manager at the publisher's address.

Library of Congress Cataloging-in-Publication Data Available.

ISBN 0-7603-0465-3

Printed and bound in Italy by New Interlitho

Front jacket (illustration by Andrew Dibben):
P&O's 70,000-ton *Oriana,* commissioned in 1995, continues the tradition
of the great liners as she cruises year-round from Southampton.

Back Jacket (photographs reproduced courtesy of William H. Miller):
(Top left) In 1965 there were only four cruise-ships sailing in summertime to
Alaska; by 1997 there were over thirty.
(Top middle) Marlene Dietrich aboard the *Normandie* in 1938.
(Top right) Posters romantically conveyed images of far-off destinations. This poster
shows the *Empress of Japan* (1930), the fastest liner on Canadian Pacific's
trans-Pacific service between North America and the Orient.

CONTENTS

ACKNOWLEDGEMENTS

It took almost the same time to produce the television series 'The Liners', including writing this book, as it did to build and launch the Queen Mary. And it wouldn't have happened at all without the support, encouragement and faith of a number of people, scattered around the world. To those listed below, and to the many more whose names do not appear but who contributed so much to the production, my sincere thanks for helping me turn a dream into reality.

My thanks to Geoff Barnes for encouraging me to research and develop the project, as it 'hadn't been done before'; David Noakes at the Australian Film Finance Corporation for support and advice in getting the project financed; Mark Hamlyn, ABC Australia; John Willis, Channel 4, UK; and Steve Cheskin, The Learning Channel, USA, for committing to the series. I would also like to pay special tribute to the team of international authors, maritime historians and economists who so willingly provided the heart and colour of our story: Bill Miller, Frank Braynard and John Maxtone-Graham in the USA; Sir Robert Wall, Ian Johnston, Professor Tony Slaven, Tom McCluskie in the UK; Jean-Paul Herbert in France; and Arnold Kludas in Germany.

Many shipping lines and their staff gave the project great support. My special appreciation to Kay Davidson and Stephen Rabson, P&O London; Micky Arison, Bob Dickinson and Joe Farcus, Carnival Cruise Lines; Doug Smith, Cunard; Princess Cruises, Orient Line, Norwegian Caribbean Line, Hapag-Lloyd, the French Line, Disney Cruise Line, Chantiers de L'Atlantique; and John S. Rogers, World City Corporation.

Chris Davies and Robert Jackson were magnificent in making the British Pathé News archives available, and special thanks to Ron Saunders for sending us such amazing footage. Thanks also to Simon Willock, Primetime, London, who put this package together and provided a base for me in London. To our producer at The Learning Channel, Adam Eisenberg, my appreciation for his professional comment and understanding.

To my friend and colleague in California, Tom Horton, who worked unceasingly to raise finance and encourage international pre-sales, and to Jean and all at THA, my heartfelt thanks for support during this project. John Coleman, an ex-BBC documentary producer, who with his depth of knowledge of the subject and his many kindnesses made working in the UK an absolute pleasure; and special thanks for his considerable contribution to this book. Calvin Gardiner, our Director of Photography, created superb pictures and provided the backing of Acme's post-production facilities. Chris Hooke took over the camera in the UK and Europe. My special thanks to Campbell McAuley for a great job as sound recordist (and for not letting his father carry heavy boxes on location), and to our Production Manager, Glenda Carpenter, for mothering us all through two extensive international shoots. Thanks to Peter Kaldor for writing such wonderful music for the series; to Rowan McAuley for patient research, and for teaching me to use a laptop; and to my wife Anne for giving me unfailing support during the many frustrating years it took to realize this project. To Susanna Wadeson and Katy Carrington at Boxtree/Macmillan, London, to writer Dick Gilling who worked with me to meet (or almost) a very tight deadline. And to Bill Miller for his understanding, for access to his amazing picture collection, for his infectious enthusiasm, great humour and knowledge as consultant on the book, a special word of sincere appreciation and gratitude.

Very importantly, a special tribute to two people without whose support 'The Liners' television series, and this book, would never have been produced: to Robert Albert for the very tangible support he made available and his continuous interest, encouragement and astute comments on content and style. Finally, to director/writer and editor Peter Butt I would like to express my heartfelt appreciation for his wisdom, patience, creative talent and unflagging support of the project during its entire life. He took my concept and turned it into reality, adding a very special magic of his own on the way.

OPPOSITE:
The 69,000-ton *Oriana*, P&O Cruises' new flagship, heading for Sydney on her maiden, around-the-world voyage in 1996. The first cruise liner designed and built specifically for the British market, *Oriana* symbolizes over 160 years of design and technological development of ocean liners and the commitment to cruising by P&O, one of the world's oldest and most respected shipping lines.

INTRODUCTION

It was a clear, cool morning with a stillness in the air, a beautiful morning, which gave promise of a typical, hot January summer's day in the making. On the top of the rugged cliffs that form the entrance to Sydney Harbour a small, enthusiastic crowd waited. Binoculars scanned the eastern horizon, appearing magically as the pre-dawn first light slowly dissolved away the veil of darkness hiding the vast swells of the Pacific Ocean.

Inside the harbour the wake of the first ferries of the day wove intricate trails of white on the dark, still waters. A small fleet of pleasure craft – all under power – headed towards 'The Heads'. Then, silhouetted against the rising sun, the great ship appeared. Within seconds the crowd on the cliffs spotted her, steaming proudly down a path of gold created by the very first rays of the morning sun. On her bow, the name *Oriana*, and, a little further aft, the letters 'P&O'.

A gaggle of television news helicopters buzzed around the giant liner like bees around a honeypot, the staccato beat of their wirring blades drowning the cheers of the onlookers as they swooped, climbed and hovered in a carefully choreographed aerial ballet, each searching for the right angle for the perfect picture. Along the rails, and from the balconies of hundreds of luxury cabins, the passengers on *Oriana* had a privileged view of their magnificent new ship's spectacular entrance into Sydney Harbour.

Water cannons on tugboats spewed great arches of water skywards in a salute of welcome to the giant visitor. Once past the spectacular opera house, with a backdrop of the harbour bridge, *Oriana* slowed almost to a stop as the tugs took over to ease the great ship safely into her berth at Circular Quay.

The early morning traffic streaming over the bridge almost ground to a halt as drivers slowed to catch a glimpse of this wonderful new 'annex' to the city skyline. By lunch time it seemed that the entire population of Sydney had descended on Circular Quay to see *Oriana*. In the evening, a thrilling fireworks display to honour the liner brought the entire harbour to life, and tens of thousands of excited Sydney-siders joined in the celebrations.

The amazing reception *Oriana* received in Sydney confirmed our research for the television series, and certainly my own belief, that the public's interest in passenger liners is as much alive today as it has ever been. The real question is why. What is so fascinating about these giant ships which appear from beyond the horizon, stay in port for a fleeting moment and then sail away, waved goodbye with as much emotion as had greeted their arrival?

Perhaps the spectacular welcome *Oriana* received in Sydney was as much a tribute to what she symbolized in the history of this island continent as it was to simply a new ship on her maiden voyage around the world. Here was a giant liner that unexpectedly stirred deep-rooted emotions in the hearts of the people of this historic port city. And Sydney is little different to New York, Halifax, Auckland, Cape Town, San Francisco or any of the world's seaports when it comes to paying homage to the role passenger ships played in the development of the New World.

For almost a century, liners transported tens of millions of people to new lives and took successful immigrants home again for family reunions; they carried the mail, and were the one and only link between the Old World and the New. They also represented the country whose flag they proudly flew. For a homesick German, Pole, Italian, Briton or any other national in a foreign land, the sight of a ship bearing the flag of their nation was a proud and emotional moment.

Our quest to unravel and explore a globally shared fascination for ocean liners, and to determine the role these giant ships have played in the last 150 years or so of world history, has been a unique and exciting voyage of discovery in its own right. It has taken our film team on an incredible journey to the historic ports and shipbuilding centres of the world. We have interviewed internationally recognized liner historians and authors; academics in maritime economics; owners and executives of today's largest cruise lines; liner captains (past and present), officers and crew; ship designers and architects; and of course, passengers who have travelled on the great liners of the past as well as the cruise-ships of today. We have been privileged to travel on the inaugural voyage of the world's first 100,000-ton cruise liner, *Destiny*, and to experience at first hand life on board a luxury, floating resort – and have also been privileged to have had a glimpse of the giant liners planned for the future, floating cities that dwarf even the largest of today's huge cruise liners.

In ports around the world, we learnt how the lives of entire populations for generations had revolved around liners: the building of them, their service and operation in peacetime and in war. We visited monuments erected in honour of those who had died in the great liner tragedies, gaining a moment of understanding of the effect the loss of a ship, its crew and passengers had on a community.

Underlying all these experiences in the major port cities and shipbuilding yards of the world, we discovered a much more powerful and significant story waiting to be told: the story of the power games and the international politics behind the financing of so many of the great liners of the past, and of the roles played by Kaisers, kings, presidents and dictators as well as the entrepreneurs who cleverly manipulated governments to finance ships ostensibly for peace and profit but which were, in reality, ships designed for war. The story of ocean liners is a saga of bitter rivalry between the various lines and, more significantly, between nations. It is also the story of the biggest migration of people in world history, of demographic change made possible through steam-powered passenger ships.

Liners became pivotal to the outcome of two world wars, and have played a major part in armed conflicts over the last 150 years or so. The 1980s Falklands War, between Britain and Argentina, was a classic case of the unique, logistical importance of liners in conducting a successful war in a remote region. Two of the world's great liners, Cunard's *QE2* and P&O's *Canberra*, carried the British troops halfway around the globe, became their base, their refuge, their hospital and, eventually, after victory was achieved, their transport home again. Even today's cruise liners, we learned, are on standby for war duties should the need ever arise.

It was with the insight we gained through visiting so many historic sites prominent in the history of ocean liners, and our discussions with many of the world's leading authorities on passenger liners, that the editorial line for the television series, 'The Liners', and this book, emerged. Our aim has been to present far more than the usual, well-chronicled 'floating palaces' aspect of transatlantic liners. The global story of great passenger ships deserves much more than that, and it is our sincere hope we have been able to add a little more depth and understanding, through both the television and this book, of an incredible maritime era and the story of the ever-evolving technology that has produced the ocean liners.

Critics who predicted the end of the great passenger ships once jet airliners were introduced were completely wrong. How many times did experts confidently predict that there would never be a liner built to rival the 83,650 tons of Cunard's *Queen Elizabeth*? In 1996, the incredibly successful Miami-based Carnival Cruise Lines introduced *Destiny*, the world's first 100,000-ton liner – with a sister ship already on order. In 1997, P&O's Princess Line launched an even larger liner, *Grand Princess*. At 104,000 tons she will be, for a moment, the biggest passenger ship ever built. But that honour won't last for long. Royal Caribbean Cruises have placed a $1 billion order for two 130,000-ton liners to go into service in 1999. At the turn of the century the contest between lines to own and operate the largest ship in the world produced amazing leaps in design, marine technology and company profits. Now the race is well and truly on again. With each day that passes, the dream of the *America World City*, a 250,000-ton floating metropolis, appears more and more feasible to finance and build.

Today, more people are travelling the oceans of the world on liners than ever before. As the renowned maritime historian and author Frank Braynard told us, 'We may see that now is just the beginning, instead of the end, of the great liner period'.

CHAPTER ONE

THE
CLASSIC ERA

On 27 September 1825 George Stephenson's steam train, *Locomotion*, shattered the peace of the north-eastern English countryside as it thundered along wrought-iron rails between Stockton and Darlington. It was the first-ever passenger train, heralding the beginning of a land-based transport revolution that would rapidly transform the civilized world. Human ingenuity had harnessed steam, making it possible to travel faster than ever imagined on land. It was now only a matter of time before this same technology could be adapted successfully for use in ships. In the early 1800s that day was not far off.

THE TRIUMPH OF STEAM

Those early decades of the nineteenth century, when the first chapter in the story of ocean liners was about to be written, was certainly a fascinating period in world history. Britain, the centre of the great Industrial Revolution that had begun in the 1760s, was consolidating its vast empire, reinforcing its global claims through dominance of the seas. Great naval victories over the fleets of France earlier in the century had earned a place in history for Nelson and Collingwood and the Union Jack flew proudly from the mastheads of the most powerful fleet of sail-driven fighting ships the world had seen. The British Empire's vast chain of colonies encircled the globe and, for over a century, holding together, communicating with and defending such isolated territories depended entirely on sail.

Throughout Britain and Europe the Industrial Revolution had created enormous social, economic and technological changes. With this change came great upheavals in the lives of millions of people. Farming communities became industrialized and traditional land-based wealth was coming under challenge by a newly emerging middle class. The era of wealthy factory owners and financial entrepreneurs had arrived. Unskilled rural labour flocked to the cities searching for work, creating unemployment on a scale never before dreamt of. In this volatile environment, greed and social injustice began to emerge. The oversupply of labour led to gross exploitation of adults and children alike and many were also affected by political and religious persecution. For a great number of people there seemed little hope for the future and, as the century progressed, the situation worsened.

On the other side of the world there was a different story. The newly independent United States of America needed people to help develop the country, to build the railroads, staff the factories and provide the services in new cities and towns. It was the same in Canada, the Cape territories of South Africa, in Australia and New Zealand. The greatest gold finds in global history were about to be made in these vast new lands. There was little wonder the 'New World' was attractive to millions in Britain and Europe. The great obstacle was the lack of cheap and reliable transport to carry them across the oceans to begin a new life in these countries.

OPPOSITE:
The packet-steamer *Eagle* passes Greenwich en route from London to Margate in 1824. Operated by the General Steam Navigation Company, she was typical of the early steamers that operated passenger services on the rivers, estuaries, and along the protected coastal waters of Britain and Europe, long before steam took over from sail on the major transoceanic routes around the world.

It was only a matter of time before steam technology combined with iron and, eventually, steel hulls, would provide the answer, creating a revolution in transoceanic travel that would bring about a huge migration of people. The newfangled 'floating tea kettles' (as the early steamships were dubbed by the sailing-ship fraternity) soon challenged the open seas, in spite of critics and cynics who believed they were destined purely for use in the protected waters of rivers, estuaries and lakes. Like the development of all new technologies, once the initial breakthrough was made, it was not long before it seemed that every engineer in the world was travelling down the same path. The momentum of change in developing and refining steam propulsion for ships was amazing.

Since the earliest days of the steam revolution, in the mid-1700s, engineers and shipbuilders scattered around the globe had been searching for the 'magic formula' that would enable them to use this new source of power in ships. If coal-burning fireboxes that heated a kettle full of water to boiling point could provide the power for locomotives to pull trains at break-neck speed across the countryside, surely this same power could be adapted to turn paddle-wheels that could propel a ship through water. The concept of paddles was not new: it had been talked about by the ancient Egyptians more than a thousand years before. It was extraordinary just how widespread research and development into steam power for maritime use was. In workshops around Britain, Europe and the United States, engineers began designing and building engines and paddle machinery for the ships of the future.

The French had one of the very early success stories. On the River Seine in 1783, Claude François, Marquis de Jouffray d'Abbans, delighted the assembled crowd by 'steaming' across the river in a little side-paddler called *Pyroscaphe*. At Lambeth, on the banks of the River Thames in England, within sight of the Houses of Parliament, Henry Maudslay, maker of precision tools, was turning his hand to marine steam engines. He would produce some of the finest and most successful of the early era. And, in 1801 in Scotland, William Symington developed a coal-fired engine to drive the stern paddle-wheel of a small river-boat called *Charlotte Dundas*.

Just over a decade later, in 1812, Henry Bell, a Scottish hotelier, installed a steam engine in a small river-boat hull. With this radical, smoke-belching paddle-wheeler, which he named the *Comet*, Bell began a regular passenger and cargo service on the River Clyde – a river that, by the turn of the century, would become the undisputed shipbuilding centre of the world. To Henry Bell and his *Comet* goes the honour of establishing the first regular steamship service in the world – a very humble beginning for an industry destined to play a major role in world history.

Four years later, in November 1816, the first German steamship, *Prinzessin Charlotte*, began operating on the River Elbe. Although the hull was locally built, her single-cylinder engine came from the Boulton & Watt works in Birmingham, England. British engineers were leading the way in the development and manufacture of steam engines for use in ships. By 1818, Italy had the first steamer in the Mediterranean, the three-masted *Ferdinando Primo*, which operated from Naples to Genoa.

The story of the extraordinarily talented American, Robert Fulton, and his role in the development of early steam-driven craft is worthy of a special mention. Born in the United States in 1765, Fulton began his working life as an apprentice jeweller. He then became a professional portrait and landscape painter, and eventually realized that he wanted to be a full-time marine engineer. At the age of thirty-two he moved to Paris to live, devoting the next four years to designing submarines; he tried to persuade Napoleon that these were the French answer to British dominance of the seas.

In 1801 the French government awarded Fulton a grant to build and demonstrate a prototype of his submersible craft. His revolutionary vessel was propelled underwater by a hand-cranked propeller, and above water by a sail mounted on a collapsible mast. In a demonstration to officials in the harbour at Brest, Fulton dived his craft, *Nautilus*, below an old, moored schooner, attached an explosive charge to its hull, and blew the schooner to smithereens. In spite of the success of this demonstration the

A replica of the *Comet*, built in 1811 by the Scot, Henry Bell, on display in Greenock, Scotland. The original was accredited as the first steam-powered vessel on the Clyde and the one which introduced steam navigation to Europe and the UK.

French ministry officials were not impressed.

In frustration and disgust, Fulton headed for England, and a meeting with the British Admiralty. The result was a similar total lack of interest. It was during this time in England that Fulton journeyed to Scotland, met William Symington and was invited to be a guest on board the *Charlotte Dundas* on her maiden voyage. It was obviously a memorable experience for the American guest. Disillusioned with the lack of interest that his submersible craft had received from the British Admiralty, Fulton packed his bags and returned to the United States where he received a similar negative response from the US Navy officials.

This decided Fulton to give up designing submarines. Inspired by his Scottish experience on the *Charlotte Dundas*, he then turned his brilliant engineering skills to developing the *Clermont*, a steam-driven paddle-wheeler. Designed to operate on the Hudson River between New York and Albany, it was built, launched and went into service in 1807. The *Clermont* was powered by an engine built by Boulton & Watt. The success of the *Clermont*, and his previous sortie into the world of naval craft, led Fulton into designing yet another radical vessel for naval use. He designed and built the world's first steam-driven warship: a 38-ton vessel with central paddle-wheels, named USS *Dermologos*. This remarkable vessel, armed with 24 x 32lb (9.6 x 12.8kg) guns, was, like the submarine before it, years ahead of its time and found little acceptance by the sail-powered navies of the world, particularly by the extraordinarily blinkered attitude of the British Admiralty. As the First Lord of the Admiralty, Lord Melville wrote, 'Their Lordships feel it is their duty to discourage to the utmost the employment of steam vessels as they consider that the introduction of steam is calculated to strike a fatal blow to the naval supremacy of the Empire.' So much for the vision of the British Sea Lords!

It was therefore not surprising that all design and development work associated with steam-powered ships for almost the entire first half of the 1800s was carried out in privately owned shipyards by commercially motivated marine engineers. Research and development finance came largely from private pockets and from shipping companies that could foresee huge profits in the future of steam propulsion.

In the late seventeenth and early eighteenth centuries, along the muddy banks of the River Thames within a stone's throw of the heart of London, in Portsmouth, Plymouth, and a dozen other river estuaries around England, master shipwrights continued to build wooden-hulled sailing ships. These vessels were the ultimate in design and craftsmanship, built within easy reach of great forests of oak and elm trees and a ready source of skilled labour by men with a heritage of knowledge developed over centuries of building some of the finest wooden ships afloat. With the coming of steam, shipbuilders and designers were faced with the dilemma of either staying with design principles practised for centuries, or making a radical move into learning the new skills and techniques demanded by the introduction of steam technology. It was as difficult a decision then for many of those skilled artisans to make as it has been for many people today to put aside pen and paper and adapt to using computers.

Sailing-ship hulls were certainly not designed to have huge engines fitted, or to have suitable additional space for enormous amounts of coal. The weight factor, plus the vibrations caused by the combination of engine and paddles,

created problems. Once an engine and all its associated machinery was installed in a sailing-ship hull, the centre of gravity changed dramatically. The delicate balance between masts, sail and the hull, and the characteristics of the sailing ships under extreme sea and wind conditions, had been fine-tuned over centuries of slow, painstaking development. Now, almost overnight, that knowledge became all but useless.

It was soon engineers rather than shipwrights who were designing the new steamers. The transition for this change was drawn out over a long period and caused considerable heartbreak and bitter argument around the waterfronts of the world. So, at this stage in our story, an insight into some of the fundamental differences between sailing ships and the early steamers may be of help in appreciating the challenge faced by the builders and designers of steamships.

The biggest disadvantage of sailing ships was the impossibility of running to schedule. They were entirely at the mercy of the elements; although the wind was free and, in good conditions, sailing ships could travel great distances at reasonably high speeds, their arrival date in port was always a guess. Just as it was impossible to know when a sailing ship would arrive, so its projected departure date was equally impossible to determine.

This uncertainty, plus the great length of time they took to complete a voyage if the weather was unfavourable, made sailing vessels a very tenuous communication link between ports, and between nations. With the expansion of colonial empires, the increase in trade generated by the Industrial Revolution and the development of the New World countries, particularly North America, regular, fast and reliable communication links across the oceans of the world became a commercial necessity. It was also essential for national governments to have regular, dependable and, most importantly, confidential communication links with their colonies and foreign representatives. This was a particular concern of the British government with its vast chain of colonies spread around the globe. With the coming of steamships – more reliable than sailing ships – governments were later to realize the inestimable benefits to be gained from being involved with their national shipping lines, particularly for the security that ships flying their own flag offered for the carriage of mail and documents of state.

For over a century, holding together the British Empire, and communicating with and defending its isolated territories depended entirely on sail. Britain's communications with India, for example, had relied on a precarious combination of sail and horse-drawn carriages for a very long time. A letter to India would travel via a government sailing packet to a French port, then go overland by horse-drawn carriage through France, then by another sailing packet across the Mediterranean, overland again across Egypt to the Red Sea and finally by sail in a vessel of the East India line to Calcutta or Bombay. The carriage of confidential communications across foreign lands, particularly those of old enemies like France, raised very real concerns of commercial and strategic security.

However, steamship designers and engineers had myriad problems to sort out before they were able to adapt the basic railway locomotive engine successfully for use in ships. The main difficulty was not so much the engine, but rather the giant, side-mounted paddle-wheels. In calm, flat water they worked reasonably well. In the swell and turbulence of the open ocean it was a very different story, particularly when paddles and sails were used in combination. The problem was fundamental. Sailing ships are designed to heel to the wind, developing their maximum speed and power as they surge down waves, through swells, with their decks presenting anything by a steady platform. The paddle shafts, mounted on these wildly bucking decks, made it impossible for the paddles on both sides to bite into the same depth of water at the same time. If one wheel was deeply submerged (with enormous strain on the shaft), and the other churning the air hopelessly, it was almost impossible to steer a ship on a steady, straight course. The enormous strains created by this imbalance in load posed severe problems that engineers had to contend with.

Another problem was the salt deposits that built up inside the boilers through the use of seawater. This required the engines to be stopped while the salt deposits were removed, a fairly long and tedious task that always seemed necessary when the engine was needed most – in a dead calm, or more often, when strong headwinds and rough seas made the sails ineffective and headway impossible. One of the very early breakthroughs in steam technology was the invention of condensers that created fresh water out of seawater, overcoming this difficulty.

The evolution of the marine steam engine is itself a long and fascinating story of dedicated engineers searching for increased power and efficiency for every ton of coal consumed. However, there is only room here to mention briefly the early development stages, from the simple side-lever engines perfected by Scottish engineer Robert Napier and Henry Maudslay in London through to the more complex, compound engines that reduced coal consumption by almost half for the same amount of power. The problem was not how to develop power but how to do it efficiently.

Once steam propulsion systems had been developed to the stage of being reliable and reasonably efficient and iron hulls began to take over from wood, the centres of shipbuilding (not only in Britain, but throughout the entire shipping world) changed. The close proximity to forests and traditional artisans were no longer major factors. The basic needs for building steamships were close proximity to iron and steel-works, coalfields, engineers and deep-water ports that could accommodate very large ships. It was a slow and at times painful move that builders of wooden ships had to face if they were to stay in business. As new shipbuilding areas were established, many of the old yards disappeared for ever.

This time of great change was, however, also a period in which many of the greatest sailing ships were built. Ironically, the last commercial use of many of the mighty square-riggers would be to carry coal to fuel the furnaces of smoke-belching steamers. In fact, in 1869, the P&O line alone had 170 sailing ships on charter carrying coal for steamers operating on its eastern routes.

Before steam-powered vessels were considered capable of making long ocean passages, a real effort was made by a shipping company based in New York to establish a regular, scheduled service across the North Atlantic. The Black Ball

Line tried to do this in 1818 with a small, three-masted sailing packet, the *James Monroe*, offering regular sailings between New York and Liverpool.

On a snowy day in January 1818, the small 424-ton *James Monroe* sat alongside pier 23, on New York's East River, preparing to sail across the treacherous North Atlantic. It was midwinter, the worst possible time of the year to make such a crossing, and there was little wonder she attracted a mere eight passengers for this historic voyage.

As the *James Monroe* swung out into the East River and as her crew shovelled away the snow from her canvas sails, well-wishers stood along the Manhattan pierside to wave a fond farewell. The Black Ball house-flag fluttered in the cold air. Down below she was a comfortable ship, her passenger quarters being described as 'extensive and commodious'. In her saloon, slabs of Egyptian porphyry supported a decoratively carved arch, and chairs with black haircloth seats ranged the length of a gleaming mahogany table. Her state-rooms (then called 'sleeping closets') were 7sq ft (0.7sq m) in dimension and were panelled in satinwood. For the month-long trip, the passengers had to contend with flickering candles, rattling water jugs and chamber pots in small closets. The meals included daily baked bread and freshly killed meat. Aiming to please the passengers her

The *Savannah* set out in 1819 from Georgia, USA, to Liverpool, England. She was the first ship ever to use steam-powered propulsion during a crossing of the Atlantic.

owners hoped to attract, the *James Monroe* was virtually a floating barn – there were sheep and pigs on board, egg-laying hens and two cows in order to provide fresh food.

Whether it was the midwinter weather for the inaugural voyage, or faults with the ship itself, the venture was a financial failure. However, the *James Monroe* sailed into a place in maritime history as the first packet to sail, rain or shine, sun or snow, full or not full, on a set day and on a scheduled service.

In spite of that shaky start, scheduled sailings quickly multiplied and competing ships became not only larger, but faster, better fitted and more comfortable. It was a bold effort by the sailing-ship owners to provide a commercial service across one of the most turbulent oceans in the world by making use of a dying technology. The odds were against them, but they tried hard. The average sailing time for the crossing was about twenty-two to twenty-five days, depending on the size of the ship and the weather during the voyage. Attracting passengers to fill these scheduled sailings became a challenge in itself. A year after the first 'scheduled' crossing by the *James Monroe*, an event of even greater historic importance took place.

In May 1819, a small sailing packet, the *Savannah*, fitted with an auxiliary steam engine and a pair of collapsible paddle-wheels, set out from her home port in Georgia, USA, for Liverpool in England. A trail-blazer in every sense, she was the first ship with steam-powered machinery to cross the Atlantic. In fact, she 'sailed' many hundred more miles than she 'steamed'. Only 80 hours of the total 663 were spent under steam. But her distinction as the Atlantic's first steamship remains intact to this day, and her departure date, 22 May, is duly recognized in the United States and observed as National Maritime Day.

However, the early interest in ocean passages under steam was by no means restricted to the Atlantic run. In 1822 a privately funded Steam Committee was set up in London to raise finance for an experimental steam voyage to India. Its major interest was the establishment of a faster, more reliable line of communication between Britain and its incredibly rich and strategically important colony. Two routes were considered: one via the more sheltered waters of the Mediterranean, with an overland link to the Red Sea and then by a second steamer to India; the second via the much longer and rougher passage around the Cape of Good Hope, a route that would require only one ship. Not surprisingly, because of the cost involved and the uncertain nature of the experiment, the committee decided on using the one ship alternative. A second Steam Committee in Calcutta, consisting of wealthy British merchants, fully supported this decision. They had a vested commercial interest in the Cape route, hoping it would reinforce Calcutta as the major British port in India. At the time, Bombay was beginning to challenge Calcutta for this distinction. Both British and foreign businesses were finding Bombay, on the west coast, more attractive for their interests and with even more potential than Calcutta on the east coast. Bombay certainly had an advantage for all shipping trade operating across the Red Sea to the Suez. Even before the canal was built and, with several alternative overland routes from the Mediterranean to India under consideration, Bombay was geographically far better situated to prosper as the major Indian port than Calcutta, the old seat of British government rule. On the other hand, for ships operating from Britain to India via the Cape of Good Hope, there was very little difference in the overall distance either to Bombay or Calcutta.

On 16 August 1825, the 500-ton *Enterprize* left London for Calcutta. On board were seventeen passengers, including 'a number of females' (the records add no further details of who they were, or why they were travelling on this voyage). In the Bay of Biscay, *Enterprize* encountered a severe gale and the amount of coal on board weighed her down deep into the water. These conditions greatly reduced the efficiency of the paddles, although the real problem was associated with the best use of the crew. It seemed that whenever they were needed for trimming the sails (and in gale conditions this was very frequent) they were down below, furiously stoking the boilers!

After a long, rough and very unpleasant voyage, *Enterprize* entered Cape Town Harbour, claiming the honour of being the first steamship to have made the voyage from

Brodie Willcox (1786–1862), the founding joint Managing Director of P&O: a clever and experienced London shipbroker who provided the perfect partner to his more flamboyant and younger partner, Arthur Anderson. (Oil by T.F. Dicksee, 1850)

and the general feeling was that, on such long voyages, steam still had a long way to go before it could successfully compete with sail. The sheer weight of coal a ship had to carry was enough to greatly diminish the performance of the early steamers and, with their lower-pressure boilers continually blocking up with salt deposits and paddle-wheels fighting a losing battle against rough seas, those early hybrid sailing/steamships had great difficulty on the long sea routes in matching the sailing clippers of the era. Whereas steam was in its infancy, sail was now at its peak in design and performance.

A less-documented voyage, but a very significant milestone in the history of steam, was the 1830/31, 148-day journey of the *Sophia Jane* from London to Sydney. This tiny side-paddler, only 126ft (38m) in length, became the first steamer to make the epic 11,000-mile (16,500-km) journey to Australia. The voyage by the *Sophia Jane* was especially important for the history of ocean travel. Only sixty-one years earlier, Captain James Cook, who travelled in a converted collier, the sailing barque HMS *Endeavour*, had discovered the east coast of Australia and claimed it for Britain. Just a short time later, this small steam-powered paddler established the first steam link between Britain and Australia.

It is difficult to compare the pioneer steam voyages across the Atlantic with those to South Africa, India, the Far East, Australia and South America. The Atlantic run had the potential for high-volume passenger traffic across a short stretch of ocean whereas, on the other routes, the volume of traffic would be infinitely smaller, but the distances involved and the logistical problems faced by pioneer steamship companies opening up these longer routes were tremendous.

It was not until 1833, fourteen years after the *Savannah*'s historic voyage in 1819, that the next crossing of the Atlantic by a steamship was made. The 370-ton *Royal William*, owned by the Quebec & Halifax Steam Navigation Company, left Nova Scotia on 17 August, bound for London. Among the investors in this venture were the Cunard brothers, Samuel and Joseph. They already ran a successful shipping business in Halifax, Nova Scotia. Samuel Cunard could see the future

England. Coal had been sent ahead for refilling the bunkers and after ten days of refuelling, the ship set sail for India. On 7 December 1825, the *Enterprize* finally arrived in Calcutta.

It had taken the steamer 103 days to make the 11,000-mile voyage. Forty days were spent entirely under sail, 62 under steam, and the remaining 10 days at anchor, loading coal. There was a great sense of disappointment among the Calcutta merchants about the time this voyage had taken, of steam, and his interest in the *Royal William* was, perhaps, more to gain knowledge of this new technology than it was to make money from his investment. However, it would be another five and a half years before Cunard, through a stroke of good fortune, would have the opportunity of making his move on the North Atlantic. This Quebec-built steamer became the first vessel to cross the Atlantic primarily under steam. On her historic, 22-day voyage, *Royal William* carried 7 passengers, a full bunker of 300 tons of coal, and 'a small amount of cargo'. She is recorded as having steamed for almost 75 percent of the trip, which included stopping the engines on every fourth day to clean salt deposits from the boilers.

As steam technology developed, more and more shipping owners began to realize the potential profits in establishing successful steamship services. Those who persisted with sail would soon be left behind. In five remarkable years, between 1836 and 1840, the most significant and exciting developments in the early history of transoceanic travel by steamships took place. It was a period of exciting technical development, of huge capital investment by shipping entrepreneurs – and a time when the British government finally accepted that awarding mail contracts to privately owned steamship companies was more practical and far more economical than persevering with poorly run, unreliable government sailing packets. It was also a period that saw the establishment of two shipping companies that still survive today, P&O and Cunard. P&O would flourish in the eastern trade, but the first commercial battle between rival shipping owners would be fought on the North Atlantic.

On almost every day somewhere in Britain during that five-year period, vital decisions were made and events affecting the future of steamship navigation were taking place. Great advances in technology were happening in the shipbuilding yards and engineering workshops, and entrepreneurial shipping owners were anticipating the potential profits steamships could earn on the sea lanes of the world.

In 1836, Junius Smith, an American lawyer/businessman

LEFT:
Arthur Anderson (1792–1868). A one-time Shetland Island 'beach boy', he was the co-founder of the P&O Line with Brodie Willcox. His flair, foresight, and imagination saw him become Managing Director and then Chairman of P&O. (Oil by T.F. Dicksee, 1850)

BELOW:
The *William Fawcett*: the chartered steam paddler which Willcox and Anderson used to open their first service between England, Spain and Portugal in 1835 under the name of the Peninsular Steam Navigation Company. (Oil by S.D. Skillet, 1836)

living in London, raised the capital to form the British & American Steam Navigation Company. Smith foresaw a regular service, with no less than eight ships operating on the transatlantic run between England and New York. The new company placed an order with London builders, Curling & Young, for the *Royal Victoria* – a wooden paddle-wheeler of about 1,900 tons – the first steam-powered passenger 'liner' to be specifically designed for the North Atlantic run and, at that stage, by far the biggest steamship ever ordered.

At the same time an extraordinary man, destined to play a major role in the development of passenger liners, entered the race. While still building the Great Western railway, Britain's most brilliant and innovative civil engineer, Isambard Kingdom Brunel, convinced the directors of the railway to extend their company's London to Bristol rail service 'all the way to New York' by building a radical new steamship to his design. After much heated discussion they finally agreed, and in June 1836 formed the Great Western Steamship Company. Their ship would be named the *Great Western*.

In a London office, a young shipbroker, Brodie Willcox and his partner, Arthur Anderson, a colourful, adventurous character from the Shetland Islands, were planning to expand their fledgling shipping business. Their interest was not on the Atlantic but on the shorter run between England and the Iberian Peninsula. These plans followed the success of their early speculative venture in 1835, when they opened a service between England, Spain and Portugal with a chartered steam-paddler, the *William Fawcett*. Their company, Peninsular Steam Navigation, had ambitions to establish a regular steamship service to Spain, Portugal and 'beyond'. Later 'Orient' would be added to their name, which would soon become known as simply P&O.

The following year, in 1837, Junius Smith's British & American Steam Navigation Company's plans for the *Royal Victoria* to be the first steamship to cross the North Atlantic from England to New York faced certain failure when their Scottish engine builder was made bankrupt. They immediately began negotiations with the St George Steam Packet Company to charter their Irish coastal steamer, the *Sirius*, a 700-ton side-wheel paddler built the previous year by the Menzies yard in Glasgow. Smith's, and his British & American Steam Navigation Company's, hopes of being the first company to offer a steam service to New York now depended entirely on the well-found – but as yet untried on the open oceans – side-paddler, *Sirius*.

In the same year, on 19 July in Bristol, Brunel's *Great Western* was launched amid great ceremony and then towed to London to have her engines installed. She was a magnificent sight and, with one of the strongest wooden hulls ever built, an outstanding product of British shipbuilding skills. The Great Western Steam Ship Company seemed unassailable in the race to have their ship the first to make the east–west crossing to New York under steam.

On 22 August, Brodie Willcox and Arthur Anderson signed a historic contract with the Admiralty to carry mail on a new service inaugurated by their Peninsular Steam Navigation Company: from Falmouth, England to Virgo (Spain), then to Oporto and Lisbon (Portugal), next to Cadiz (Spain) and, finally, Gibraltar. This was the first government mail contract ever awarded to a private shipping company operating steamships. It was a real breakthrough that would influence the entire history of passenger lines, particularly in the area of owners raising finance for building and operating steamships capable of fulfilling stringent government contract requirements.

Prior to awarding the mail contract to Willcox and Anderson, the British Post Office had been forced to rely totally on the Admiralty and their sailing packets for the overseas delivery of all communications. These ships, armed for defence against any warship or privateer attack, were also used as training vessels for seamen and elderly officers for whom the Admiralty had to find jobs no matter how incompetent or inefficient they were. It was a situation that neither the Post Office nor the commercial sector found at all satisfactory. The services provided under these extraordinary circumstances were slow, irregular and unreliable. Willcox and Anderson saw the business potential on the Iberian Peninsula route for a more regular and cost-effective service. Knowing that the Post Office was tired of the Admiralty arrangements and that the private sector would welcome a faster, more regular service, they lobbied the government for a contract to carry the mail on this route, but were turned down.

However, as their Peninsular Steam Navigation Company was already running a successful service from Falmouth to Oporto, Portugal, and return, it was not difficult for Willcox and Anderson to organize a clever public relations campaign to further their cause. They arranged regular reports to the press of the striking performances of their company's outward- and inward-bound steamers. Under the heading 'March of Steam', one leading paper reported:

> The IBERIA steamship, belonging to the Peninsular Company, sailed from Falmouth on 22nd May and arrived off Oporto on the 25th, IN 66 HOURS. The BRAGANZA, belonging to the same Company left Oporto on the 25th and arrived in Falmouth on the 28th IN 70 HOURS, bringing letters from the IBERIA's passengers. So that in 136 hours, or something SHORT OF 6 DAYS from their leaving England, advices of their safe arrival in Portugal were back in England.

The pressure of public opinion and the outspokenness of business circles, carefully and skilfully massaged by articles like this, forced the government to rethink its decision. Public tenders were called for the provision of a regular mail service, to be operated by steamships over the exact route proposed by Willcox and Anderson.

Two tenders were received by the Admiralty, one from the Peninsular Steam Navigation Company and the other from the British & Foreign Company. There was obviously a dislike

The Irish coastal steamer *Sirius*, under charter to Junius Smith's British & American Steam Navigation Company, became the first steamship to make the east-west crossing of the North Atlantic.

Isambard Kingdom Brunel's *Great Western*, built for the Great Western Steamship Company, on her departure from Bristol to New York in 1838. (Engraving by Joseph Walter)

within government circles for the situation forced on them by Willcox and Anderson and, for a moment, it looked as though they would not be awarded the contract. This situation changed immediately it was made public that the British & Foreign Company had neither the ships nor the means to meet the terms of the contract. The Peninsular Steam Navigation Company, after a prolonged delay, was finally awarded the contract, which was duly signed on 22 August 1837.

The Post Office was delighted, immediately announcing cheaper postage rates on this route. The success of this first private mail contract was significant in the history of the development and the financial future of all British passenger lines. It changed the system from a total monopoly by Admiralty-controlled sailing packets to a tendering system whereby commercial steamship companies could bid for a contract to carry overseas mail.

Obtaining a mail contract became an essential ingredient for commercial success, the financial cornerstone on which many of the world's great passenger lines in future years relied. A mail contract provided and guaranteed the cash-flow costs of building and operating the ships, the passengers provided the profit. It was a simple financial equation that worked.

No one understood this equation better than Brodie Willcox and Arthur Anderson. Prior to being awarded a contract in 1837, their company had weathered a very tough financial period. Without the contract they may not have survived, but with it they were able to expand and develop their operation into what was to become one of the world's largest and most successful shipping lines.

On 28 March 1838 the steamer *Sirius*, on charter to Junius Smith's British & American Steam Navigation Company, sailed from London bound for Queenstown, Cork, on the southern coast of Ireland, to take on passengers, mail, and as much coal as she could possibly carry, before setting out for New York. On 4 April, with 40 paying passengers and 450 tons of coal on board, *Sirius* steamed out of Queenstown Harbour to begin the long passage across the North Atlantic. She was ahead of her rival *Great Western*, which was still tied up in Bristol, making last-minute preparations for the voyage.

Four days after *Sirius* sailed, on 8 April, the *Great Western*, with smoke billowing from her single tall stack, steamed out of Bristol in hot pursuit of her smaller rival. On board were only seven passengers, enjoying the unprecedented luxury of the 'supership' of the era. On 22 April *Sirius* arrived in New York after an eventful voyage during which the crew ran desperately short of coal, forcing them to burn cabin furniture, plus an emergency mast, to maintain steam pressure in the boilers. Her passage time was 18 days, 10 hours at an average speed of 6.7 knots. She was the first steamer to make the east–west crossing of the North Atlantic.

Great Western steamed into New York only 4 hours after *Sirius*. Her time for the crossing – 14 days, 12 hours – made her almost 4 days faster than her smaller rival. Parties, parades, salutes and ceremonies celebrated the safe arrival of both ships. To *Sirius* went the honour of being the first steamer to make the crossing and to *Great Western* went the honour of being the fastest. This first-ever race between two passenger ships belonging to rival companies signalled the birth of the immortal Blue Riband, a contest between passenger ships operating on the North Atlantic to set the fastest average speed for the crossing.

In early November 1838, following two highly successful years of the Peninsular Steamship Company carrying the mail to Spain and Portugal, the British government, through the Post Office and the Admiralty, advertised in the London *Times* for tenders for the operation of a regular monthly North Atlantic mail service by steamer. Both the St George Steam Packet Company, owners of the *Sirius*, and the Great Western Steam Ship Company, successful operators of the *Great Western*, submitted proposals.

The advertisement in *The Times* caught the eye of a London-based friend of Samuel Cunard. He dispatched a copy quickly to Cunard in Halifax, together with an attached note containing the short but prophetic message: 'This is for you'. The interest of the 51-year-old Nova Scotian, already an extremely successful and wealthy businessman, was immediately fired by this unexpected opportunity to achieve his dream of establishing a regular steamer service across the Atlantic with British government financing. Samuel Cunard, without hesitation, decided to go to London to bid for the contract.

On arrival in London, Cunard received the good news that the Admiralty had rejected the proposals submitted by the two British companies. In a borrowed office in Piccadilly, Cunard, a man accustomed to dealing with government bureaucracies, prepared a simple, straightforward proposition:

> I hereby offer to furnish steam boats of not less than 300 horse power to convey the mails from a point in England to Halifax and back twice in each month. Also to provide branch boats of not less than 150 horse power to convey the mails from Pictou to Quebec and back while the navigation is unobstructed by ice – the whole arrangements to be subject to such restrictions and directions as the Lords of the Admiralty may think proper to introduce into the contract.
>
> For the performance of this service I am to receive the sum of £55,000 per annum, to be paid quarterly for the period of 10 years and after the expiration of that time six months notice of discontinuance to be given by either side, and in consideration of the length of time the contract is to continue, should any improvements in steam navigation be made during the continuance which the Lords of the Admiralty may consider as essential to the service, I do bind myself to make such improvements and alterations as their Lordships may direct.
>
> The Boats to be in readiness to convey the mails on 1st May

Samuel Cunard, founder of the Cunard Line. A successful Halifax, Nova Scotia shipping owner, Cunard won the first British Government mail contract to establish a regular steamship mail service across the North Atlantic.

1810 but I am in hopes to have them ready sooner; every exertion shall be made to accomplish it – the contracts to commence on 1st May or earlier if the boats are ready.

On 11 February 1839, a tired Samuel Cunard hand-delivered this proposal to the Admiralty. They passed it on to the Treasury for comment. Within days the document was returned to the Admiralty endorsed: 'The sum is not unreasonable if the Lords of the Admiralty are prepared to entertain a proposition of this kind.' The Admiralty advised Cunard that they were, indeed, prepared to commit to such a proposal. It was a historic moment, and Samuel Cunard was delighted. Now he had to find the best engine makers and shipbuilders in Britain, firms capable of delivering the highest-quality vessels on schedule and on budget.

Through a long business association with the East India Company, Cunard arranged a meeting with the company's Secretary, James Melvill. 'The one man you should talk to', Melvill advised Cunard, 'is Robert Napier, the Glasgow engineer who built the engines for our paddler, *Bernice*.' Accepting this advice, Cunard wrote to Napier. Within days, Samuel Cunard and Robert Napier met, established an immediate liking and respect for one another, and came to an agreement. Napier would build three ships of 800 tons, each fitted with the latest 300hp engines, for £30,000 each. Napier made a note in his diary that the price he offered Cunard was extremely competitive, 'with a view to future orders for the like'.

Napier's first design indicated the need for a larger engine to cope with the long transatlantic crossings, which in turn meant larger coal bunkers. He revised the design, coming up with an entirely new vessel of 960 tons, to be driven by a 375hp engine. The cost of this new concept was £38,000, which Napier offered to Cunard for £32,000 per ship.

On 18 March 1839 Cunard signed a contract with Robert Napier to build the ships, all agreements between them being subject to final Admiralty approval. By 4 May the formal contract between Samuel Cunard and the Admiralty was finally signed. It included a number of amendments to the original proposal and also contained stiff penalty clauses for failure to meet specific terms of the agreement.

Napier conducted extensive trials of the new design he had submitted to Cunard and was not satisfied with the results. He recommended an increase in the overall length of the hull and modifications to the paddle-boxes, measures he felt were necessary to improve the seaworthiness of the ships and the speed that was required to meet the terms of the contract. These modifications would, of course, cost more. He advised Cunard by letter that he would honour his contract to deliver the ships on schedule as per the original agreement, but added a strong rider that he advised against this course.

Alarmed, Cunard once more sought the advice of his friend James Melvill at the East India Office. 'If you accept what Napier says about the requirements of the ships you need, put your cards on the table and see what he suggests,' Melvill counselled. Cunard agreed and headed for Glasgow where, through Napier, he met a small group of potential investors including the Burns brothers, George and James, who ran a successful small fleet of paddlers, their partner James Donaldson, and David MacIver, agent for the City of Glasgow Steam Packet Line.

For four days the group went over every aspect of what Cunard was proposing, time and time again. They finally agreed and Cunard disclosed his plans to form a new company to run the operation, to be called the British & North American Royal Mail Steam Packet Company. The capital required was pledged from Glasgow-based investors. Samuel Cunard became a 50 percent partner, George Burns and David MacIver shared the other half of the mail contract, plus a further half share in the ships to be built. For this percentage they paid £25,000, with a proviso that they could raise the balance of the capital required. It was also decided to build a fourth ship. With the new company and the partnership agreements in place, a relieved Cunard returned to London for what he hoped would be final talks with the Admiralty.

Meanwhile Junius Smith's *Royal Victoria*, completed at last and renamed the *British Queen*, sailed from London on her maiden voyage to New York on 10 July 1839. At that time she was the largest steamship in the world at 1,862 tons and 254ft (76m) in length. A second giant steamship for

Smith's British & American Steam Navigation Company, the 2,366-ton *President*, was launched in Limehouse, London, and then towed to Liverpool (they tried to sail her to Liverpool but she proved to be unmanageable). Junius Smith was determined to capture the bulk of the ever-growing North Atlantic passenger trade but, unlike Willcox and Anderson, and Samuel Cunard, Smith's company had no mail contract to subsidize the huge expenses of running an international shipping operation. The financial gamble associated with running such a precarious business venture would eventually bankrupt him and many other companies in this early era of steamship development.

On 4 July, at a meeting with the Admiralty in London, Samuel Cunard won agreement for an increase in the annual subsidy to cover the cost of the larger ships recommended by Robert Napier. With all details of the amended contract now agreed, the three partners went their separate ways to prepare for the new venture. Cunard returned to Halifax on the second voyage of the *British Queen*; David MacIver left for his home in Liverpool to prepare the groundwork for the new operation; and George Burns remained in Glasgow to supervise the building of the first four 'Cunard' liners.

Two weeks after Samuel Cunard's successful meeting with the Admiralty, on 19 July 1839 in Bristol, the iron keel of the most radical steamship of the era was laid. It was the latest creation of Isambard Kingdom Brunel. If they hoped in the near future to win the mail contract awarded to Samuel Cunard with his fleet of four new steamers, the Great Western Steamship Company knew they needed three ships at least equal in size and speed to the *Great Western*. However, inspired by the success of his first ship, Brunel convinced the directors of the company to build, not the three new vessels they needed, but one 'real giant of a ship'. The new vessel would be almost twice as big as any before it, with its hull constructed from iron plates rolled to shape and riveted together. Too big and heavy to be constructed on a conventional slipway, it would be constructed in a dry dock. Its motive power was planned to come from the largest paddle-wheels ever constructed; its length would exceed 300ft (90m) and its gross tonnage would be 'around 3,000'.

As no shipyard was prepared to tender for such a radical vessel, the Great Western Steamship Company took on the job themselves. They secured waterfront land almost in the heart of Bristol where the dry dock was constructed and contracted William Patterson, builder of the *Great Western*, to supervise construction of the 'giant'. The ship would be appropriately named *Mammoth*.

In early January 1840 Samuel Cunard boarded the *Great Western* for yet another long winter voyage back to England. He would travel on to Glasgow to be present at the launching of the *Britannia*, the first of his new company's four ships. At Greenock, on the River Clyde on 5 February, Robert Napier's daughter, Isabella, officiated at the launching of Samuel Cunard's new company's first steamship, the *Britannia*. It

The Royal Charter of Incorporation of The Peninsular and Oriental Steam Navigation Company, dated 31 December 1840.

was a proud day for the locals as this steamship, designed and built on the Clyde, and with its engines also made there, rolled down the heavily greased slipways to begin life afloat. With a sense of 'more to come', the cold but clear Scottish day echoed with the cheers of the shipbuilders, their families and the party of officials present for the ceremony. It was a memorable day for Samuel Cunard, witnessing not only the launch of his first ship but also the birth of a new line destined to bear his name proudly on the oceans of the world.

If there was one man in Britain who seemed destined to create great ships and great lines by the sheer power of ideas, it was Isambard Kingdom Brunel. In May 1840, with construction of his successor to the *Great Western*, the *Mammoth*, well under way, a small, experimental vessel, the 237-ton *Archimedes*, arrived in Bristol to demonstrate its newly designed screw propeller, the brainchild of Kentish farmer-turned-inventor, Sir Francis Pettit Smith. Brunel, anxious to gain first-hand knowledge of this revolutionary propulsion system, chartered the *Archimedes* for private trials. Delighted with what he learned, he decided to change the design of his new ship from a side-wheel paddler to the first propeller-driven steamship ever built for ocean passages. It was also decided to change the ship's name to the *Great Britain*. Her success both on the Atlantic and, later, on the vastly longer run to Australia convinced Brunel that big ships had great advantages over small vessels, particularly on long, open-ocean passages.

In late June, Cunard's *Britannia* arrived in the port of Liverpool to prepare for her maiden voyage. Little fuss was made of the new ship's arrival; no claims were made that she was the 'biggest', the 'fastest', or 'the most luxurious' ship afloat. She was none of these, but was simply a fairly large, well-founded new side-paddler, designed, built and engined on the Clyde in Glasgow. The local press only spared two lines to announce the arrival of *Britannia* in Liverpool.

On Saturday 4 July, at noon, sixty-three passengers, including Samuel Cunard and his daughter Ann, embarked by ferry from Liverpool's Pier Head to board *Britannia*. Sharp at 2pm, Captain Henry Woodruff, RN, headed his fine new ship downstream towards the open ocean. *Britannia*'s destination was Boston in the United States, via Halifax, Nova Scotia.

On 17 July, *Britannia* reached Halifax after a voyage of 11 days, 4 hours, and on 20 July the Boston crowds went wild with excitement as the *Britannia* berthed at the newly designated 'Cunard Wharf'. Her voyage was considered by many prominent Bostonians as 'the most significant crossing of the Atlantic since the *Mayflower*'.

From the moment the *Britannia* arrived in the USA, the distance across the Atlantic was effectively almost halved, and the sense of isolation the people of this port city felt from the 'Old World' was enormously diminished. It was no wonder the people of Boston cheered, and elevated Samuel Cunard to almost folk-hero status – such was the impact of the steamship on Boston, and not long after, on the world.

The British government was delighted with the success of the mail contract with the Peninsular Steam Navigation Company, and sought a preliminary proposal from Willcox and Anderson for the extension of the mail services to Egypt and, possibly, India. In good faith they responded to this request, setting out full details and requirements for such a service by drawing on their experiences. The government then used this very specific and confidential information as the basis to call public tenders for the contract to carry the mail between England and Egypt! Four tenders were received. The lowest, and most practical, proposal was submitted by Willcox and Anderson. The government accepted their tender.

On 31 December, the last day of 1840, the British Royal Charter of Incorporation of the Peninsular and Oriental Steam Navigation Company was signed, sealed and delivered. With a new management structure in place, and a working capital of £1 million, joint Managing Directors, Brodie Willcox and Arthur Anderson, and their 'P&O' Line, planned further expansion of their steamer services, beyond Egypt, via the Cape of Good Hope to India and, eventually, to Hong Kong, Japan, Singapore and the fast-growing British colonies, Australia and New Zealand. While the ships of Samuel Cunard were about to dominate the North Atlantic, P&O had already established itself as the premier shipping service to all ports 'east of Suez'.

In an amazingly short period, between 1836 and 1840, great leaps were made in maritime steam technology and shipbuilding techniques. The size alone of the ships being built and planned had more than doubled. Steam engine technology had overcome many of the major drawbacks of the original auxiliary engines that were installed in sailing ships converted to paddle-wheelers. Comparing the wooden-hulled *Savannah*, designed and built in New York as a sailing ship at 320 tons and 100ft (30m) in length with a 90hp, single-cylinder engine, saltwater boilers and collapsible paddle-wheels, to Brunel's *Great Britain*, the first passenger steamer with an iron hull, a screw propeller, a balanced rudder and waterproof bulkheads, was like comparing a 1940s DC3 aircraft with a 747 jumbo jet. At 3,270 tons and 289ft (87m) in length the *Great Britain* was the most revolutionary ship of the era, the true forerunner of the great iron and steel-hulled liners of the future.

The design of engines was very much the key to the development of bigger, faster and more reliable steamships. Early low-pressure, single-cylinder engines had evolved to powerful, giant, twin-cylinder machines with side-lever units fitted in pairs to turn the shafts, and the enormous paddle-wheels. The *Great Britain*, for example, was an ingenious, four-cylinder, 1,000hp monster, operating on steam pressure

Brunel's revolutionary *Great Britain*, launched from her building dock in Bristol on 19 July 1843 by HRH Prince Albert. She was the 'wonder-ship' of the age, the forerunner of the modern ocean liner.

OPPOSITE:
The mighty *Great Eastern*, five times larger than any vessel ever built, ready for launching in November 1857. Brunel's colossus, the largest man-made object designed to move ever built, lay on two timber cradles resting on 120 iron rollers that straddled 160 railway lines. These were on a 2ft bed of concrete, supported by 2,000 timber piles driven 10m into the gravel bed of the River Thames. Only on the highest of high tides was there any possibility of a successful launch. Moving over 12,000 tons of dead weight had never before been attempted.

of 15lb per sq in (1kg per sq cm). Its 7ft 4in (220cm) diameter cylinders formed a pair of inverted Vs, the drive to the propeller shaft being transferred via a multiple chain-drive system. Designed by Brunel's father, it was the most radical steam engine of the decade.

As the size of the ships and their engines became larger and larger, the amount of coal they needed to carry increased dramatically. But with the increases in size, hull designs evolved to incorporate bulky engines and huge coal bunkers while still leaving proportionately greater space for passenger accommodation and cargo. Whereas *Savannah* had two reasonably well-furnished state-rooms and berths for 32 passengers, the *Great Britain* boasted accommodation for 360 passengers in state-rooms and cabins, and had the largest and most lavishly appointed main dining saloon afloat.

While smoke from the early steamers was beginning to darken the skies above the sea lanes of the world, hard-driven sailing packets were crossing from Liverpool to New York in twenty-three days or so, about a week longer than most of the early steamers. Passengers requiring berths on the much longer routes to India, the East, and to distant Australia, New Zealand and South America were still largely choosing sailing ships because, in most cases, the cost and frequency of these ships made them a far more attractive proposition than their rivals with engines.

In the mid-1800s, while the British had a head start in the race for dominance of steamship technology, along the banks of the East River in New York an estimated 10,000 shipwrights and riggers were turning out the fastest sailing ships of all time, the famous Yankee clippers. It was the same in Boston, and between that port and New York, upwards of forty new clippers a year were being launched.

The major shipbuilding centres of Britain were in a similar situation. On the Thames, the Clyde, the Mersey and a dozen other such rivers, the last of the famous British sailing ships were being built alongside the controversial new steamers. Most sail traditionalists considered the steamship as nothing but a 'flash-in-the-pan' maritime experiment. One day soon, they hoped, the steamers would disappear, leaving the oceans

Brunel (second from right) hardly left the site during the three months it took to launch the *Great Eastern*. 'The Little Giant', as he became known, supervised every launch attempt. With him are the builder, John Scott-Russell (left), Henry Wakefield (with plans) and Lord Derby.

free once more as highways for wind-jammers, clipper ships and sailing packets.

It was a time of dramatic maritime transition, the beginning of a slow but inevitable process that aroused passions and saw epic contests waged on the open ocean as sail threw out its last challenge to the smoking steamers. The real irony was that, for many of the magnificent sailing ships, their last commercial use would be transporting coal to fuel the very ships that eventually would bring about their obsolescence. And as time went on, with even greater ignominy, many of these proud ships, with their masts, rigging and bowsprits removed, were permanently anchored in remote ports scattered around the world as floating coal hulks in which the black fuel for steamers was stored.

The lure of the Atlantic endured. In 1846, four years after the Cunard Line began its North Atlantic services, an American, Edward K. Collins, owner of a successful fleet of sailing packets, set out to gain the US government's financial support to establish a mail service to operate in direct competition to Cunard. A colourful and successful character from Cape Cod, Collins had a number of things in his favour. He was a great talker, a friend of people in high places in the government, and already the owner of a profitable shipping line operating along the east coast of America. Collins also loved a gamble, and the high stakes at risk in running a passenger line service across the Atlantic appealed to him.

In 1847 he convinced the US government to sign a mail contract with his new company, the New York & Liverpool United States Mail Steamship Company, to carry US mail between New York and Liverpool on a schedule of twenty round trips a year. To achieve this, he would commission five new steamships, equal to or better than any other vessels afloat, to be designed and built in American yards. The US government was delighted to have the opportunity of competing with British interests for supremacy on the Atlantic, and backed Collins with a guaranteed subsidy of $385,000 per year.

The notion of challenging not only Samuel Cunard's successful mail service on the North Atlantic, but also British supremacy on the high seas, was dear to the heart of many influential members of the US government. 'We have the fastest horses, the prettiest women and the best shooting-guns in the world, and we must also have the fastest steamers,' stated Ohio Congressman, Edson Baldwin Olds. [1] Senator James Baynard, jun., from Delaware added his unequivocal support to the government's plans to finance the Collins line on the basis that it would 'proceed with the absolute conquest of this man Cunard'.

Collins set out to do just that, in luxuriously appointed

ships designed to capture the passenger market from the very spartan Cunard ships which, although they were fast winning a reputation for reliability and punctuality, provided very few comforts for their passengers. His four new ships, *Atlantic*, *Pacific*, *Arctic* and *Baltic*, all designed and built in New York, were around 500 tons heavier and 2 knots faster than the Cunard vessels. Interior woodwork was of the finest polished timbers; heavily carpeted drawing-rooms featured luxury armchairs and sofas; the ceilings were carved and gilded and the tables fitted with Italian marble tops. Huge ice-rooms kept food fresh, and the menus rivalled those of the top New York and European restaurants.

If Cunard had built his reputation on reliability and the somewhat austere facilities his vessels provided for passengers, then Edward Collins would introduce style and luxury for those travelling on the ships of his line. For the first time on the North Atlantic there would be a clear choice for passengers to make between the ships and the services offered by two rival shipping companies.

On 27 April 1850, the *Atlantic* sailed from New York on its maiden voyage with over 100 passengers on board. After an eventful voyage that included very rough weather and numerous technical problems, she arrived in Liverpool on 10 May to be greeted by a very enthusiastic reception. Visitors flocked to view the splendour of this new Atlantic steamer. Cunard, it appeared, had a very serious rival to contend with if the *Atlantic* was an example of what the new Collins Line had to offer. *The Illustrated London News*, which reported the new ship's arrival, also noted that, 'The *Atlantic*, as well as other vessels building for the same line, are so constructed as to be converted into vessels of war in a few days, should necessity require.' There was obviously a proviso in the contract Collins had signed with the US government requiring dual-purpose use for the vessels, a quid pro quo for their dollar investment.

In 1852, with all four ships operating, the Collins Line was living up to its boast to outdo its Cunard rivals. In eleven months it carried over 1,300 more passengers than Cunard and, in most cases, made the crossing in less time. But the running costs to achieve these results were extremely high,

and the US government was called on to double its annual subsidy to keep the company going. The biggest cost problem was associated directly with both Collins' and the government's insatiable quest for speed. 'Speed!', urged Delaware's Senator Baynard, 'Speed of such magnitude as the Government of Britain and its chosen instrument, this man Cunard, never visualised or could ever hope to achieve'.[2]

Pacific became the first steamer to make the westbound crossing in under ten days, but the cost of these high-speed runs was slowly but surely sending Collins' company into financial ruin. The damage to engines continually run beyond their design limits, the expense of the coal and the maintenance required on the wooden hulls after each voyage all contributed to these high costs. Added to this was the labour required to maintain the high level of service that the line boasted, making the whole operation a financial nightmare. Even with double the original government subsidy, the line was operating at an ever-increasing annual loss.

Then came tragedy. On 20 September 1854 the *Arctic*, with 233 passengers on board, including Edward Collins' wife and two children, collided with a small iron-hulled French steamer. The wooden-hulled *Arctic* sustained severe damage and sank off the Newfoundland coast in dense fog. In all, 322 lives were lost, including Mrs Collins and her children. Only eighteen months later the *Pacific*, en route from Liverpool, disappeared with the loss of 45 passengers and 141 crew.

Apparently undismayed by these tragedies and mounting financial problems, Collins ordered a new wooden-hulled side-paddler, the *Adriatic*. The decision to build in wood rather than iron came at a time when the Cunard line had already decided to adopt iron for all their ships. Launched in April 1856, *Adriatic* was larger, at 3,650 tons, and faster than any other ship of the period, and was the largest wooden-hulled steamer ever built. She was also more luxurious than anything else afloat, with accommodation for 375 passengers. But instead of saving Collins, she caused him financial ruin.

The government cut back its annual subsidy, as author Frank Braynard explains:

They were the finest ships in the world for about a decade, but the southern congressmen and senators, whose votes were necessary to get the subsidy money, were even then fearing and worrying about the coming Civil War. They said, 'What are we doing? We are subsidising northern shipowners to build vessels which could be used against us as troop ships should there ever be a Civil War.'

Lack of subsidy, the sheer cost of running this new ship and the ageing and tired *Atlantic* and *Baltic* caused the creditors to step in and close down the Company. As one journalist writing in *Harper's Magazine* summed up this US challenge to British dominance of the North Atlantic run, 'We had best stick to sailing ships and leave steam navigation of the ocean to John Bull.'[3]

As early as 1853 Brunel's iron-hulled, propeller-driven *Great Britain* was operating a fast and efficient service between England and Australia, carrying up to 630 passengers on each voyage. For almost twenty years this 'mother' of all modern ocean liners continued to provide regular services between Liverpool and Melbourne. On one voyage, in 1861, *Great Britain* carried the first all-England cricket team to visit Australia. The one drawback Brunel felt this radical ship suffered from was its need to take on coal a number of times on this 11,000-mile (17,600-km) voyage. He planned to overcome this in his third and most famous ship, which would eventually be named *Great Eastern*.

Work started on building the *Great Eastern* in 1854 on the banks of the River Thames at Millwall. Five times larger than any ship before her, *Great Eastern*'s size and the sheer audacity of her design shook the shipping world. She was 693ft (208m) in length, 120ft (36m) in width (including paddle-boxes), with a Gross Registered tonnage of 18,915 tons. Her engines, totalling 2,600hp, drove two side paddles, each 58ft (17.5m) in diameter, plus a single 24ft (7.2m) screw propeller. Her masts could carry some 6,500sq yd (5,435sq m) of sail. There was a double-hull construction technique for safety and electric light planned for the mainmast that would 'bathe the ship in perpetual moonlight'. She would carry 12,000 tons of coal – enough to make the journey to Australia without refuelling. On board, for comfort, there were berths for 4,000 passengers (more than twice the number carried on the 83,000-ton *Queen Mary*, which went into service in 1936). It took 2,000 workers almost four years to create *Great Eastern*, and after many financial problems her owners went bankrupt and she was sold to a consortium called the Great Ship Company. They placed her on the England to New York run, not on the long haul to Australia and the East that she had been designed for.

On this infinitely shorter run, *Great Eastern*, after her early mechanical problems had been overcome, proved to be a technical marvel but a financial disaster. On her maiden voyage to New York in June 1860, she carried only thirty-eight paying passengers, in spite of the heavily reduced cost of tickets for the crossing. Potential passengers cancelled in large numbers following the continual delays in the sailing date. It seemed also that the very size of the vessel alone frightened people from venturing to sea. Her greatest promotion asset, it appeared, became *Great Eastern*'s biggest drawback. It took a crew of over 400 to run the ship and the fuel costs alone on some voyages exceeded the income from paying passengers. She never sailed with all berths filled – in fact, the most passengers she ever carried was in 1861 when, under charter to the British government, she had on board 2,144 officers and men, 473 women and children and 122 horses bound for Canada. On this one voyage *Great Eastern* carried over 3,000 people – a record number for one ship that would not be exceeded until the First World War.[4] The *Great Eastern* was financially doomed. Her creator, Brunel, did not live to see what a failure his colossus was. He suffered a severe stroke and died only eight days after *Great Eastern* sailed on her sea trials.

The Great Ship Company went into liquidation in December 1863, and *Great Eastern* was sold and chartered to the Telegraphic Construction and Maintenance Company where she spent the most useful years of her life laying telegraph cables across the Atlantic and, later, from Bombay, India, across the Red Sea to Aden. With this task completed, Brunel's colossus spent her last days as a floating amusement park moving around the sea ports of England, Scotland and Ireland trying to earn her owners a last few dollars before her final trip to the breaker's yard in 1888. During her entire life afloat, *Great Eastern* remained the largest ship in the world, a technological masterpiece, decades ahead of her time.

The Cunard Line preferred to make haste slowly. It was 1852 before Cunard ordered their last wooden vessel, the paddle-steamer *Arabia*. In 1855 they commissioned their first iron vessel, the *Persia*, built by the Glasgow builders, Robert Napier & Sons. *Persia* swept across the Atlantic in July 1856 in 9 days, 1 hour, 45 minutes at a record average speed of 13.82 knots. The Blue Riband, for the fastest time across the Atlantic, previously held by the American Collins Line's *Arctic* now belonged to *Persia*, the first iron-hulled steamer on the Atlantic run.

Five years later, in 1861, the last paddle-driven ship of the Cunard Steamship Co., *Scotia*, was launched. She was another magnificent ship built and engined by Robert Napier. *Scotia* smashed the record time across the Atlantic and held the coveted Blue Riband for five years between 1862 and 1867. Her last crossing for Cunard, in September 1875, signalled the end of the era of paddle-wheelers for the line she served so well. In the year that *Scotia* won the Blue Riband, 1862, Robert Napier delivered Cunard's first screw-propelled liner, *China*.

In 1865 Sir Samuel Cunard died. He had been created a baronet in 1859 for services to the British Empire and he was, without a doubt, the founding father of successful passenger lines across the North Atlantic.

THE SINEWS OF EMPIRE

In 1841 Anderson suggested to the British government that a canal linking the Mediterranean and the Red Sea through Suez would be a great asset. It was not until twenty years later that retired French diplomat and engineer Ferdinand de Lesseps consolidated plans for digging the Suez Canal, a giant, imaginative project that would greatly affect the politics and power bases of every nation with interests in the Mediterranean region, and in the riches that lay 'east of Suez'. Over five precarious, frustrating years, de Lesseps lobbied and negotiated, cajoled and manipulated in order to persuade the French, British and Egyptian governments to share jointly in the cost of building the canal. Of all the countries that the canal would benefit, Britain was the

hardest to convince. Prime Minister Palmerston completely refused to be part of the scheme, pointing out that the government had already committed heavily to the building of a railway line linking Port Suez on the Red Sea with Cairo and Alexandria on the Mediterranean.

The British could see an easy passage to the East via a canal by the ships of all nations as a threat to British supremacy in India and beyond. While her ships ruled the waves, British dominance of the sea lanes on the long route to the East via the Cape of Good Hope was the greatest safeguard of Empire she could have. A canal, they reasoned, would rob Britain of this great maritime advantage, making it possible for rival nations to gain easy access to the wealth of the East. Also, as the proposal for a canal was made by a Frenchman, and a major portion of the finance would be French, the British government, in principle, were opposed to investing in a joint venture with their traditional rival. But after years of wrangling and clever negotiations, de Lesseps formed a company, raised the capital through public share issues and, with the active and financial support of the Egyptian authorities, began the enormous task of digging the canal. There was no British investment.

On 17 November 1869, the Suez Canal was officially opened amid pomp and ceremony unparalleled in that area for centuries. Empress Eugénie, wife of Napoleon III, Emperor of France, officially opened the canal; national leaders and aristocracy from Britain (although the government still officially opposed the canal), Europe and the Mediterranean countries attended the week-long celebrations; and a convoy of ships of all nations, including P&O's wooden paddle-steamer *Delta*, began the historic three-day voyage of celebration, from Port Said on the Mediterranean to Port Suez on the Red Sea. As the convoy finally entered the Red Sea, the continent of Africa had suddenly become an island, and the sea route between Europe and the vast Pacific Ocean, with all its nations, cultures and their associated wealth, had effectively been halved in sailing time and had become instantly more accessible for the new steamships, hungry for trade. Ironically, when it opened, the country that stood to gain

The early mail route sailings of P&O from Southampton to Alexandria stopped at Gibraltar and Valetta, the harbour of Malta. (Watercolour from *Route of the Overland Mail to India*, 1850)

most from the Suez Canal, Britain, had neither a financial interest nor control in running it.

That situation dramatically changed in 1875, when the Tory Party came to power and Benjamin Disraeli was elected Prime Minister. When the unexpected opportunity to privately purchase two-fifths of the total shareholding in the Canal company arose the government acquired it swiftly for £4 million. It was a coup for Britain, negotiated and agreed without the knowledge of the French. Had they known the

shares were on offer, the French government would have almost surely snapped them up, giving them absolute controlling interest in the Suez Canal. Prime Minister Disraeli and his British Cabinet made a 'behind closed doors' decision to purchase. Disraeli broke the news to Queen Victoria, 'It is just settled: you have it, Madam. The French Government has been out-generalled.'[5]

Scheduled passenger services to India, Singapore, Hong Kong, Japan, Australia and New Zealand via the new canal became more frequent and more economical. London to Bombay, for example, was soon reduced to 15 days – a vast difference from the 113-day inaugural steam voyage to India made by the *Enterprize*. Trade was encouraged as steamers carried the products of British and European factories to the huge markets in the East. On their return voyages, tea, silks and spices, wool and wheat, the traditional goods of the sailing ships, were getting to the markets of Europe faster and more reliably than ever before.

With this burgeoning trade came great wealth and power. Trading empires, built on sail, became even stronger with the introduction of the steamers. Regular communication brought with it strategic advantages, both commercial and national. Outposts of empire became regional power bases and the very presence of these new technological marvels, the steamships, arriving and departing on regular schedules, provided impressive evidence of the strength of the nation under whose flag the ships operated. Britain had an early dominance, but soon ships flying the flags of Germany, France, Italy, Holland, Canada and the United States appeared, looking for trade, and established their own colonial interests and political alliances. All these countries were looking for their own special place on the international commercial scene.

Port Said on the Suez Canal: a P&O steamer, Jubilee class of 1887–8, enters the canal southward bound on a mail service. (Watercolour from *P&O Pencillings* by W.W. Lloyd, 1890)

35

NORTH ATLANTIC MIGRANTS AND RIVALS

In Germany in 1847, in the port city of Hamburg, a group of shipowners formed a new company to establish a service between Hamburg and New York using a small fleet of sailing ships. It was called the Hamburg-Amerika Line. In 1856 the company bought its first steamer and soon added three more to its fleet.

This line had a great rival, North German Lloyd, founded at Bremen, only a short distance from Hamburg, in 1857. The traditional rivalry between the two ancient port cities had come to a head with the founding of these two shipping companies. North German Lloyd, like Hamburg-Amerika, was soon to become one of the world's most successful and powerful passenger lines. In 1879, a young man named Albert Ballin, whose story is inextricably linked with the great migration of people from Europe to the United States, began to make his presence felt as an immigration agent in Germany. Albert was born on 15 August 1857, the last of nine children. His father, Samuel, a Jewish immigrant from Denmark, ran a fairly unsuccessful immigration agency. After his father died, Albert bought out the other partners and the business began to flourish, largely because of the ability of the young proprietor but also because at that time, in 1879, the flow of immigrants from Europe to the United States was increasing by the day.

Albert Ballin was a compassionate man. He was also shrewd enough to realize that the best way of increasing his business was for the people he handled to send back a good report of his services to others wanting to migrate. It worked, and his agency prospered. At that time, all the migrants he handled took passage on small ships to England where they were transferred to large British flagged ships for the voyage across the North Atlantic, mostly to New York. Working so closely with the British shipping companies, Ballin had a marvellous opportunity to study British ships and all the procedures for handling large numbers of migrants. He also acquired mastery of the English language. The problem with this transhipment process was that it required a second agent in England, which meant that every commission Ballin's company earned had to be shared. It became obvious that

future big profits to be made from the burgeoning immigrant trade belonged to the shipping companies which were able to offer cheap, rapid and direct passage between European and North American ports.

In 1881 Ballin, with this in mind, suggested to a young Hamburg shipbroker, Edward Carr, that two new freighters he was ordering could be readily modified to accommodate up to 640 immigrants. Ballin went on to guarantee Carr that if he would provide these two ships, his agency would fill them with immigrant passengers. They agreed, a contract was signed, and the cost of passage set at 25 percent less than steerage class fares on ships of the Hamburg-Amerika and North German Lloyd lines.

Within a year, the Carr Line had increased its fleet to six vessels, and Ballin had delivered 11,000 immigrants, with a guarantee of more to follow. This new, small line was beginning to hurt Hamburg-Amerika and North German Lloyd. A price-cutting war began. It lasted for four bitter years of wrangling and fierce rivalry until a solution came in June 1886 when the Hamburg-Amerika Line effectively amalgamated with the Union Line, the name under which the Carr Line was then operating. Under the terms of this new arrangement, Albert Ballin was appointed chief of Hamburg-Amerika's passenger division.

In 1888 Ballin became a director of Hamburg-Amerika, his influence reflected in the growing success of the company in all areas of its expanding international operations. In 1899 he was appointed Managing Director of the line. At forty-two years of age, Ballin had guided the development of Hamburg-Amerika from the world's twenty-second largest line in terms of tonnage to the largest steamship company in the world. Ballin would be arguably the most significant individual in the history of ocean liners. And at that stage, at the turn of the century, the real competition between lines and between nations for the huge profits that transoceanic travel, and particularly the immigrant trade promised, was only just beginning. It was the competition between Germany and Britain for the transatlantic trade that would be the most intense.

Between 1880 and 1924, over 26 million people arrived

on American soil for the first time, nearly all transported steerage class in passenger liners flying the flags of almost every maritime nation in the world. They left Britain, Ireland and Europe in huge numbers. For the vast majority, the land of choice was the United States.

Since the early decades of the 1800s the increase in population and radical changes in the workplace had created much poverty in Europe and Britain. The unemployed and disadvantaged had looked to the New World for hope of an escape from their deprived living conditions. Now that journey became possible. With sail, the number of berths available was limited. Steamships changed this, enabling unprecedented numbers of people to cross the oceans and begin a new life.

In the late nineteenth century British engineers and marine architects remained unchallenged as the world's leaders in the specialized business of building ocean liners. Of all the centres in Britain few could compare with the yards on the River Clyde, Glasgow. The first Cunard ships were built there and were such a success that, until the turn of the century, every nation that boasted a fleet of ocean liners relied heavily on the products of the shipyards and engineering works established along the banks of this narrow, winding Scottish river. Even if the entire vessel was not built there, then almost surely the engines and the propulsion systems would be. There was more knowledge about building liners along the River Clyde than there was in the rest of the shipping world. There were many shipbuilding companies, but none destined to make such an indelible mark on the history of ocean liners as John Brown & Co., the company that established their yards on a stretch of the river known as Clydebank and eventually went on to build some of the world's greatest liners: *Lusitania*,

LEFT:
Albert Ballin, dynamic Managing Director of the Hamburg-Amerika Line, appointed to that position in June 1897.

Aquitania, *Queen Mary*, *Queen Elizabeth* and the *Queen Elizabeth II*.

As Glasgow-based author and maritime historian, Ian Johnston, recounts, John Brown's began as simply one of the many shipbuilders located on the Clyde:

The shipyard started off in 1851 as one of some forty yards on the banks of the Clyde, right in the heart of Glasgow. They had a 4-acre [1.6 ha] site, but because of port developments in 1871 their site was compulsorily purchased and they were told to clear off! They looked for another site further down the river and, eventually, bought a little farm from a Miss Hamilton of Barnes. It consisted of 31 acres [12.4ha] right opposite the River Cart. Here they set up their yard, which became known as Clydebank Shipyard, and in time gave its name to the town – which only came into existence once the yard was established. Suddenly, from being a farm, there were two or three thousand men working there, clambering away, driving rivets. The racket must have been unbelievable for the few residents, presumably mostly cows and sheep in the vicinity.

The success of the site lay in it being opposite the River Cart, which meant that very large ships could be launched right into the mouth of this river. I'm not sure if James and George Thompson, who selected the site, recognized this, because at the time the largest ship they contemplated was around 5,000 tons and about 300ft (90m) in length. Later on, to think there'd be an 85,000-ton ship, 1,000ft (300m) long, going down the same slipways into the same stretch of river, I'm sure they couldn't have imagined.

However, John Brown's was certainly not the only British yard building passenger ships. There were rival shipyards competing for every order placed by British and overseas-based lines. It was a lucrative, highly competitive business, and winning contracts and gaining the confidence of owners did not come easily. Ian Johnston continues:

To begin with, John Brown's main opposition was from other yards on the River Clyde, but eventually Harland & Wolff's Belfast yard would probably be considered their most serious rival. But there were others, Campbell Laird in Liverpool, Swan Hunter on the River Tyne, and Vickers at Barrow-on-Furness. But I would say Harland & Wolff probably represented the most strategic threat to the development of building large ships at Clydebank. Through their Chairman, Lord Pirrie, Harland & Wolff enjoyed a special relationship with a number of shipping lines that they operated on very special terms with. In fact, it's quite likely that John Brown couldn't have been considered on equal terms.

Across the Irish Sea, the Belfast-based shipbuilding firm of Harland & Wolff was founded in 1861 through a partnership between two young men with very diverse backgrounds: Edward Harland, an English-born design engineer from a wealthy family, who had served his apprenticeship with Robert Stephenson & Company engineering works in Newcastle-on-Tyne, and Gustav Wilhelm Wolff, a draughtsman who came from Hamburg, Germany. They bought a run-down yard and started business as Harland & Wolff, a company that still exists today as the largest shipbuilding business in the UK.

With Gustav Wolff's Hamburg shipping connections, the shipyard had little difficulty in winning contracts to build the early steamers of the newly established Hamburg-Amerika Line. Their early iron-hulled ships won much praise for the quality of their construction and the many innovative engineering improvements directly attributable to the skills of both partners. An indication of their success is that, between 1862 and 1864, they built and launched sixteen ships – a new ship went down their slipways every six and a half weeks.

From the 1860s until the turn of the century the Clydebank, Merseyside, Tyneside and Belfast shipyards were all competing against one another for contracts to build bigger, faster and better liners for British owners. With additional orders from Germany, Holland, France and Italy flooding in, there was little wonder these yards became complacent about their seemingly unassailable position as the world's leading builders of ocean liners. British steam technology and engine development was virtually unchallenged as the best available.

In fact, the majority of British shipyards obviously thought that they controlled steam technology and the art of building ocean liners. When, in the last years of the nineteenth century, a German shipbuilder launched a giant 'superliner' that made every vessel produced in Britain until that time pale into insignificance, it shook the very foundations of the entire British shipbuilding industry, and the naval strategists as well. In retrospect, it should not have come as such a surprise. Since the introduction of steam-powered ships, British shipyards had welcomed visiting engineers and designers from foreign yards to come to see ships and engines being built and installed. It was all about winning new contracts.

Of course, many of the foreign owners would have preferred to have their vessels built in their own countries and, by the late nineteenth century, Germany and France in particular had expanded their shipbuilding facilities and skills to a stage where they could produce their own liners. That encouraged the 'head-hunting' of skilled professionals in all areas of shipbuilding and engine technology from the major British yards.

Foreign governments also realized the national value in developing their own shipbuilding capabilities. In that burgeoning technological age, national self-sufficiency not only made good economic sense, but good strategic sense as well. The ability to build great ships for peaceful purposes mirrored in no small way a nation's capability of also building ships for war. And as the century drew to a close, armed aggression in the name of imperial expansion policies being pursued by emerging powers in Europe was always a distinct and ever-present possibility.

In 1871, a new and powerful entrepreneur entered the North Atlantic scene. He was Thomas Ismay, a young Liverpool shipowner, who had bought a bankrupt fleet of fast-sailing clipper ships operating on the UK to Australia run. It was called the White Star Line. In ordering new ships for his newly acquired line, Ismay accepted an offer of extremely attractive prices from Harland & Wolff to build the ships in return for a minority shareholding in the White Star Line. It was very similar to the deal that Robert Napier made with Samuel Cunard three decades earlier.

Harland & Wolff later bought shares in the UK/South Africa operator, the Union Castle Line. It was a smart business move for shipbuilders to hold an equity shareholding in successful lines. This situation guaranteed the yard an inside opportunity for all the new ships the line would order. As company historian Tommy McCluskie recalls, 'Harland & Wolff had a large share of White Star, Union Castle, Royal Mail and Pacific Steam Navigation Co. and others. And as such, those companies would tend to favour their own, if you like, in-house yards.'

With the consolidation of the White Star Company came a serious challenge to every other line operating on the North Atlantic, particularly the Cunard Line. Thomas Ismay made no secret that it was Cunard and their Clyde-built ships that he wanted to beat. The first White Star ship launched in 1871 under the partner arrangements with Harland & Wolff, the *Oceanic*, rendered every other ship of the time completely obsolete as far as passenger comfort and services were concerned.

> In consultation with Thomas Ismay, the partners planned totally novel passenger accommodation. The saloon ran the breadth of the ship, allowing passengers on a transatlantic liner to eat together for the first time. A built-in smoking-room was provided instead of a canvas deckhouse. The cabins were almost doubled in size and fitted with large portholes and electric bells. These elaborate interior fittings owed many of their features to observation of large hotels, made by William Pirrie (the company's chief designer) who had been sent on a tour of England and the Continent for this purpose.[6]

It was not until 1881 that Cunard launched a ship that could compete with White Star's *Oceanic*. Their new ship, *Servia*, which entered service on 26 November that year

was, apart from Brunel's *Great Eastern*, the largest ship in the world. At 7,400 tons, 530ft (159m) in length she was the first-ever liner fitted throughout with electric light. Her steel hull and huge engine, which drove a screw propeller, gave the radical Cunard ship a speed of just under 17 knots, and earned for *Servia* the title 'Ocean Greyhound', a term that would be used for all the great transatlantic liners of the future designed specifically for high-speed passage across this turbulent stretch of ocean.

With a string of 'greyhounds' to follow, and the purchase of Guion Line's speedster, *Oregon*, Cunard had resumed mastery of the North Atlantic. Their ships held the Blue Riband, and passengers were returning to the line in droves. What was surprising was that the Cunard company was sticking with the older, compound engines while the trend of its opposition was to install the new triple-expansion engines in their new vessels. Triple-expansion engines were certainly more economical to run, but the staid Cunard management felt the tried and proven compound power plants were still the best for reliability. *Umbria* and *Etruria*, of 1885, were both fitted with compound engines designed and built by master engineer John Elder. Both vessels were able to maintain 19.4 knots, whatever the weather.

Two of the most magnificent liners built before the turn of the century were the Inman Line's (later to become the American Line) *City of New York* and *City of Paris*, the first ships to exceed 10,000 tons since the *Great Eastern*. Each had a bowsprit accentuating the classic line of their clipper-like bows, and were both indeed true ocean 'greyhounds'. With twin funnels, twin- triple-expansion engines, and twin screws, they were the fastest pair of liners of the era. In 1890, on her second voyage between Liverpool and New York and back to Liverpool, *City of Paris* smashed the speed records in both directions, becoming the undisputed Blue Riband speed champion of the Atlantic. The battle raged until Cunard took the Riband with *Campania* and *Lucania* in 1893 at 22 knots. The White Star Line gave up the contest, but fiercer rivals across the North Sea did not.

THE SHADOWS LENGTHEN

As the century neared its end, it was not only the design and technology of ocean liners that was changing. A new and powerful nation was emerging in Europe. The unification of the Germanic states followed a series of wars instigated by the Prussian Prime Minister, Prince Otto von Bismarck, a great militarist who believed that 'blood and iron' were the only means to achieve this unification. In 1864, the armies of Prussia won control of the Schleswig-Holstein part of Denmark; in seven weeks, in 1866, they overwhelmed the Austrian army, allowing Bismarck to declare a North German Confederation under Prussian rule. Finally, in 1870, Bismarck's forces defeated the French army under Napoleon III. In 1871, Wilhelm, King of Prussia, became Kaiser of a united Germany. The enormous natural resources, the size of the populations involved and the creation of a nation with vast territorial borders made unified Germany the dominant new power in Europe.

The new nation had close ties with Britain; Kaiser Wilhelm I's son, Frederick William, was married to Queen Victoria's eldest daughter. Their son, Prince Frederick William Albert Victor, was twelve years of age when his grandfather became one of the most powerful figures in Europe. In his turn he would become a figure of fear and hatred for the British, as Kaiser Wilhelm II.

On a summer afternoon in 1889, the young Kaiser was a guest at a British naval review at Spithead, off Portsmouth. As well as the great fighting ships of the British Navy, it was White Star's newly commissioned liner *Teutonic* that caught the Kaiser's eye. Even the fierce-looking British dreadnoughts did not overshadow this smart-looking ship, 582ft (174m) in length. The Kaiser was not only charmed by the high standard of her decor, but he was also fascinated by her general design and her dual purpose. With special armour added to parts of her hull and with small guns mounted on her open, upper decks, she could also serve as a wartime armed merchant cruiser. Wilhelm had an immediate vision of similar dual-purpose German liners, only bigger and faster than this White Star newcomer. Upon disembarking from the anchored *Teutonic*, he was said to

remark, 'We must have some of these.'

Now a powerful unified nation, the Germans were planning to become a major seapower. Furthermore, Germany wanted to demonstrate to the world its industrial and technological might, and planned to build such new ships not in British shipyards, but using German shipbuilders. They were to borrow skills and secrets as well as the craftsmen from the British yards and then, after mastering their skills and methods, send them home. And, indeed, the Germans did build a liner that changed transatlantic fashions for ever.

The German presence on the prestigious, ferociously competitive North Atlantic was divided between two important firms, Hamburg-Amerika Line and North German Lloyd. Neither seemed interested in big liners or transatlantic records until the 1890s. At that time, their plans and priorities changed, prompted mostly by Kaiser Wilhelm II himself, but also by the steadily increasing numbers of passengers and the pure profit potential of this expanding trade.

North German Lloyd was the first to make a move. They went to the highly skilled Vulcan Shipyards at Stettin and stated, 'Build us the fastest passenger ship in the world and we'll buy it, give us anything less, and you can keep it.' The design teams at Vulcan responded with enormous enthusiasm, creating a long, slender ship fitted with the most powerful machinery yet to go to sea and, as if proof of her potential capabilities, she was capped by no less than four tall, mustard-yellow funnels, the first 'four-stacker' ever built.

'This was a tall, fast, always fearsome-looking ship that would open a new era in steamship history,' according to maritime author and historian John Malcolm Brinnin. He continues:

It was a period when the landscapes of Valhalla inscrolled on the walls and ceilings would all but collapse under their own weight as well as a period of Teutonic efficiency united with matchless engine power that would give Germany all the honours of the Northern seas. On board, the ceilings of her public rooms were higher than those of any other ship and the walls loaded with paintings, carvings and bas-reliefs that glowed in the sacerdotal radiance of stained glass.

John Malcolm Brinnin was writing about the 14,900-ton *Kaiser Wilhelm der Grosse*, the first of a new breed of German passenger ships, and the vessel often called the 'first superliner'. The Kaiser personally attended the launching, held in May 1897, and the ship was named *Kaiser Wilhelm der Grosse* after his grandfather. She was to be palatial, luxurious – indeed a floating palace.

The *Kaiser Wilhelm der Grosse* swept the North Atlantic in the autumn of 1897. She made the run to New York in a very impressive 5 days and 20 hours, at an average speed of 22.35 knots. The Blue Riband was at last in German hands and would remain with them for the next decade. The British, and specifically the Cunard Line, were startled.

It took a couple of anxious years before a British yard launched a ship to rival the German four-stackers. In 1899, at Harland & Wolff's yard in Belfast, White Star Line's new *Oceanic* was launched. At 17,200 tons, she was larger than the *Kaiser* by well over 2,000 tons. The *Oceanic* became the 'world's largest', and among the huge crowd that came for the launching was the Kaiser himself.

The Hamburg-Amerika Line, Lloyd's greatest national rival, was also envious of the *Kaiser Wilhelm der Grosse*. Immediately, they ordered a record-breaker of their own, a larger ship than the *Kaiser* at over 16,000 tons. In 1900, this new ship, the *Deutschland*, easily took the Blue Riband. She too was a four-stacker, grand and perhaps over-gilded, and initially extremely popular. But the *Deutschland* developed problems. While she had great speed, it was at the expense of the passengers' comfort. There were vibrations, rattling and excessive noises from her soaring, steaming quadruple-expansion engines. Earlier in the decade, the otherwise highly competitive White Star Line had claimed that they were no longer interested in high speed, especially if it risked passenger comfort. Now, the mighty Hamburg-Amerika Line began to feel the same way. Hereafter, both of these major companies would emphasize comfort and luxury over record speed. While the sleek *Deutschland* managed to hold the

THE FOUR FLYERS

KAISER WILHELM II
KRONPRINZESSIN CECILIE
KRONPRINZ WILHELM
KAISER WILHELM Der Grosse

Leave NEW YORK on Tuesdays for BREMEN
Via PLYMOUTH (London) and CHERBOURG (Paris)

A poster announcing the Atlantic services for the quartet of four-stackers of North German Lloyd.

equated with size, speed, luxury and, perhaps above all else, with safety. Everyone wanted to sail in ships with several funnels and so, while the three-stackers were very popular, the four-stackers were even more so.

Between 1900 and 1914, over 12 million people crossed the Atlantic in third class and steerage. By 1914, one-third of America's population was foreign-born. Usually, the immigrants travelled in small, poorly ventilated, often claustrophobic and cramped quarters, mostly in the bowels of passenger ships. By the turn of the century, however, steerage had improved. The Hamburg-Amerika Line, under Albert Ballin's management, took perhaps the most elaborate and thoughtful measures. They created a complete immigrant village, fully equipped with a laundry, synagogue and even a brass band, to process passengers for their westbound liners. By 1913–14, in the final days of unrestricted immigration between the Old World and the New, the biggest liners, such as Hamburg-Amerika's *Vaterland*, were even fitted with steerage dining halls with uniformed stewards.

In 1902 the liner business, dominated for almost half a century by British-owned shipping lines, and now with stiff competition from German, French and Dutch lines, received a further shock from an unexpected source. The American financial tycoon J. P. Morgan formed the International Mercantile Marine and bought out no less than six British passenger-ship firms, including the well-known Red Star, Dominion and Leyland Lines. But the 'jewel' in this takeover was the entire capital stock of the mighty White Star Company, now one of the largest and most illustrious firms in the passenger business. White Star cost Morgan an extraordinary $25 million – and he paid cash for it, all in gold. Morgan, one of the richest men in the world, then failed in his attempt to acquire a German line and set his sights on none other than Cunard.

The Liverpool Head Office of the Cunard Line was alarmed. The Chairman of the Board, Lord Inverclyde, had no hesitation in seeking British government support to change the company's Articles of Association to prevent control by any foreigners. Lord Inverclyde went even further. Not only did he seek the government's help to prevent the takeover, he

prized Riband for six years, until 1906, the cost was high. She was not considered a very successful or, apart from her very early voyages, a very popular ship.

North German Lloyd soon built three other giants: the *Kronprinz Wilhelm* in 1901, the *Kaiser Wilhelm II* two years later and, finally, the *Kronprinzessin Cecilie* in 1906. These ships were extremely successful and very popular. With each successive new ship, there seemed to be more luxury, more marble and certainly more gilt. The Germans also established one of the earliest marketing campaigns for ocean liners. Very quickly, the four mighty funnels aboard each ship were also wanted a government loan to build two new 'superliners' – the biggest, fastest and most powerful two ocean liners ever built. He wanted to take on, not only Morgan and his White Star Line, but also the Germans and their ocean 'greyhounds' on terms that would ensure success for Cunard and for Britain.

Lord Inverclyde's additional argument during his discussions with the government was the possible threat of a war with Germany, a feeling growing among political and business leaders at the time. At Queen Victoria's funeral in

1901, the Kaiser and his uncle, now King Edward VII, had together mourned for the great Queen they had both loved and respected. But following his grandmother's death, Kaiser Wilhelm became increasingly envious of the Empire his uncle now ruled and his cousins would one day inherit. He had an expansionist imperial policy for Germany in direct conflict with British and French interests, and as the German Navy grew in strength under Admiral von Tirpitz, it seemed inevitable that one day the Kaiser would go to war against Britain. With this impending threat, Lord Inverclyde proposed that the two new 'superliners' should be designed and built for fast conversion to armed cruisers. In the advent of war they would add a powerful pair of high-speed fighting ships to the fleet of the British Navy.

The British government agreed to all that Lord Inverclyde had requested, including a loan of £2,600,000, repayable over twenty years at 2.75 percent interest. In addition, a twenty-year subsidy of £150,000 per annum would be paid to meet additional costs incurred in meeting the strict Admiralty requirements during the construction of the two

ABOVE:
While never intending to be the fastest, White Star Line wanted its new trio – *Olympic*, *Titanic* and, later, *Gigantic* – to be the largest as well as the finest Atlantic liners of their day.

LEFT:
The great liners and their size were often romanticized, especially when depicted in poster and postcard art. Here, the *Mauretania* appears far higher than she actually was when alongside her berth.

43

ships. After concluding this remarkable arrangement with the government, Lord Inverclyde, in a letter to a board member in August 1902, concluded by saying, 'Personally, I am satisfied, and the more I think about it the more do I consider that this is one of the biggest and most important

Sir Charles Algernon Parsons (1854–1931). In 1884 he perfected the steam turbine for use in ships, his revolutionary engines providing the power that ship builders had dreamed about in their race to build bigger and faster vessels for both peace and war.

arrangements which have ever been made between a private Company and the Government of this Country.' It would not be the last.

Orders were placed for the two 'superliners', which would be named *Lusitania* and *Mauretania*, two ships destined to play a major role in the future of the British Empire. *Lusitania* was built at John Brown's yards on the Clydebank and *Mauretania* on the Tyne by Swan, Hunter & Wigham Richardson. They were both fitted with new and revolutionary steam-turbine engines, a technological master-stroke.

In 1884, the Irish-born gentleman-scientist Charles Parsons had developed a steam turbine that successfully drove an electric generator. Ten years later he founded the Marine Steam Turbine Company, which was totally devoted to developing the steam turbine as the ultimate source of power for ships. The principle used had been understood for a long time, but Parsons was the man who perfected it. He used steam pressure to drive a series of blades mounted on a revolving shaft, connected to a screw propeller. Parsons produced enormous drive power, economically and without the vibrations associated with piston-driven engines. Frustrated after a series of rejections from the Admiralty, Parsons built his own experimental boat, called *Turbinia*, fitted his turbine engine and, at Queen Victoria's Diamond Jubilee Grand Naval Review in 1897, he made his move. With smoke pouring from the stack of the little *Turbinia*, he broke through the cordon of assembled spectator boats and headed straight down the line of anchored battleships. The naval élite present were furious, but the Parsons turbine had arrived, and days later the Admiralty relented and eventually ran trials on the engine.

The steamship lines took notice. In 1905, Cunard ran a test with two brand-new, 19,500-ton sister ships, the *Carmania* and *Caronia*. The *Carmania* was completed with new steam turbine engines; her sister had the standard quadruple-expansion engines fitted. The *Carmania* proved to be not only faster, but more efficient and economical.

As a result, both *Lusitania* and *Mauretania*, each 31,500 tons and 761ft (228m) in length, would be fitted with four

giant Parsons turbines, so powerful that they were capable of generating 75 per cent more power than equivalently sized reciprocating engines. Cunard was making sure they would be much faster than their four-funnel German rivals.

In 1907 both the *Mauretania* and *Lusitania* went into service on the transatlantic run. Cunard had a pair of winners from the moment they made their maiden voyages. On her second crossing, *Lusitania* regained the Blue Riband for Britain, but it was a short-lived triumph for the Clyde-built 'superliner'. On her maiden voyage, *Mauretania* proved to be fractionally faster than her sister ship and the Blue Riband

The mighty *Lusitania* blowing an unusual amount of smoke during her trials in May 1906. Her giant turbine engines are still to be adjusted.

passed from one new Cunard ship to another.

The *Lusitania* and the *Mauretania* were the first ships to make the Atlantic passage in under five days. Mauretania's record of four days, nineteen hours remained unchallenged – much to the delight and pride of the British and Cunard – for twenty-two years, until 1929. While there were certainly larger liners to come in the immediate years ahead, none of them had the power to outpace the remarkable *Mauretania*. Her record was finally broken by a German ship, North German Lloyd's *Bremen*, in the summer of 1929.

The *Mauretania* was one of the most popular, profitable and beloved liners of all time. 'When she was born in 1907,' said Franklin Delano Roosevelt, US President 1933–45, 'the *Mauretania* was the largest thing ever put together by man. She always fascinated me with her graceful, yacht-like lines, her four, enormous black-topped red funnels and her appearance of power and good breeding.'

The *Lusitania* and *Mauretania* were beautifully decorated, although perhaps more conservative than the heavy, wooded, over-gilded German ships. Like many British liners to follow, and in particular the Cunard ships, the overall tone was solid and reliable, not pretentious or extravagant. Cunard believed in the value of history: public rooms in Italian and Renaissance styles, restaurants in straw-coloured oak capped by glass domes. State-room styles varied: Adam, Sheraton, Chippendale. The smoking-room had a wagon-headed roof, special details copied from Italian villas and the best wood veneers made from British as well as French trees.

The steam turbine soon powered almost all ships. White Star planned a trio, the number then needed for a weekly relay between Southampton and New York; Cunard planned a third liner to join their new sisters and fill out their weekly timetable; the French would finally proceed with their first major liner; and the Hamburg-Amerika Line had the most startlingly ambitious plans of all for building a trio of successively larger 'superliners', the first to exceed 50,000 tons. The respective governments financially endorsed and enthusiastically encouraged these big liner projects. The ships enhanced national goodwill and image, and were technological as well as decorative statements – floating

ambassadors for the nations they represented.

If there was one line that wanted to outdo all its rivals, not so much in speed but in sheer size and luxury, it was the White Star Line. 'After 1907, Cunard was stealing all the glory with the *Lusitania* and *Mauretania*,' says Tom McCluskie, historian at the Harland & Wolff shipyard in Belfast. He continues:

. . . and Bruce Ismay (Chairman of White Star) invited Lord Pirrie (Chairman of Harland & Wolff) for dinner one night in London. The brandies flowed. Ismay decided he was going to have the biggest, grandest, fastest ships that anyone ever had. Through dinner, they talked of their plans. Pirrie sketched out on the back of a napkin the basic design specs for the *Olympic* and her sister, the *Titanic*. They would be the biggest ships yet, approximately 46,000 tons. Floating palaces. That thumbnail sketch was brought up to Belfast and shipyard designers told 'to put the meat on the bones'. And the *Olympic* and *Titanic* came from that.

Money was said to be no object. Ismay didn't worry about cost . . . At first, they planned to build two liners. But Ismay insisted that Cunard had two big liners and so therefore White Star must have three: the *Olympic*, *Titanic* and *Gigantic*. In fact, when Sunday dawned on them and they half sobered up, they realized that White Star could only afford two. So they went for the *Olympic* and *Titanic*, and then the third ship further down the line.

The *Olympic* was the forerunner, the prototype . . . She was the last word in luxury. Money was no object in the interior fitting of the ship. She was designed to be exactly as Ismay wanted: a floating palace. But as reality dawned, problems in actually building such ships started coming out of the woodwork. We had to build larger slipways, overhead gantries and a dry dock because there wasn't one in all of the UK big enough to take the ship. Another problem was that the river at Belfast wasn't wide enough. And so we cut a big chunk out of the opposite side of the riverbank. To this day, it is still known as Titanic Cut. We decided to build the first two liners in tandem, side by side. Because of intricate casting, plating requirements, etc., it was easier to build two ships rather than roll a plate for one ship and go back at a later date and do the same thing over

OPPOSITE:
Port bow view of *Olympic*, painted white, on the slip prior to launch, October 1910. Her sister ship, the *Titanic*, is shell-plated and in Slip No. 3.

46

again for a second ship. The *Olympic* was laid down first and the *Titanic* followed. One ship mirrored the other as construction went along. From keel-laying to launch was approximately thirteen months. And then a further five months outfitting. So you are looking at eighteen months from the very first plate going down to delivery to the owner. The *Titanic* didn't have actual sea trials because the *Olympic* was so successful. The *Titanic* simply had a few adjustment runs on her delivery voyage from Belfast down to Southampton. Another interesting point is that White Star did not launch these ships in conventional terms. There were no brass bands, no champagne bottles, no formal ceremonies. The ships were seen simply as objects. When completed, they were pushed into the water with very little if any ceremony at all.

In May 1911 the *Olympic* left her builder's berth at Belfast. She was the ultimate in design and shape, the total embodiment of all the hopes and dreams that Ismay had discussed with Pirrie over dinner in London some years earlier. Launched as the 'biggest ship in the world', she certainly was the largest British liner at the time. There were squash courts and the first 'swimming-bath' ever to go to sea. The state-rooms were decorated in no less than eleven different styles, from Italian Renaissance to old Dutch. Even the beds were noteworthy: they were said to be the widest afloat.

As the *Olympic* left Belfast, the *Titanic* took her place at the fitting-out berth. Worried that this second liner would be overshadowed by her elder sister and to give her added cachet, her owners decided to describe her as the 'world's safest ship', and claimed she was 'virtually unsinkable'. On 10 April 1912 she departed from Southampton on the most famous, most documented and most disastrous maiden voyage ever. *Titanic* made two stops before heading out across the Atlantic, at Cherbourg in France where she took on passengers (including many immigrants) and at the southern Irish port of Queenstown (now Cobh) where more passengers and mail were loaded.

At midnight on Sunday 14 April, *Titanic* rammed an iceberg in the western reaches of the North Atlantic. Within four hours the 'unsinkable' ship plunged 11,200ft (3.4km) to the floor of the icy Atlantic. An estimated 1,503 passengers and crew perished; a little more than a third, 705 in all, were saved.

To this day, controversy still rages over the circumstances surrounding this maritime tragedy. There were accusations of gross negligence by certain officers and by the ship's Master Captain. H. J. Smith, who was a highly experienced seaman making his last voyage before retirement. There were also accusations that Bruce Ismay, Chairman of the White Star Line, a passenger on board, insisted that the *Titanic* remained at full speed in spite of the warnings about icebergs the ship had received, simply to 'arrive on time in New York'. Ismay was one of the survivors; his personal behaviour during the disaster, and later during the rescue, is reported as 'leaving a lot to be desired'. Criticism of his role in the sinking haunted him until the day he died. The behaviour of the officers in preventing steerage and second-class passengers access to exits though first-class areas horrified people. In the calm seas, a ship in the area ignored flares and, later, closed down their radio for the night and missed distress calls from the sinking liner, leaving hundreds of people to drown. Among those lost were several multi-millionaires and leading international businessmen, but the stark reality was that the largest number of deaths was of those travelling steerage class. Very few of these people, accommodated in crowded quarters well below the water-line, survived. Also among those who perished was Thomas Andrews, Harland & Wolff's Managing Director and Chief Designer, responsible for the building of the *Olympic* and *Titanic*. His personal notebook contains evidence of a tragic change of plan, made under the direct instructions of the owners.

The most glaring aspect of the tragedy was the lack of lifeboats the ship carried. In the calm conditions, the majority of people would have been saved had there been sufficient boats to accommodate the number of passengers and crew on board *Titanic*. During the research for the series, in Harland & Wolff's offices, Belfast, we were allowed access to the handwritten notebook that belonged to Thomas Andrews. It was his day-to-day record of building details on both the *Olympic* and *Titanic*. Modifications and changes to the original

OPPOSITE:
Harland & Wolff, Queen's Road, Belfast with workers leaving the shipyard in May 1911. The *Titanic* can be seen in the distance in the centre of the picture. The vessel at the quay on the left is *Nomadic*, a White Star Line tender which is still in use as a restaurant in Paris.

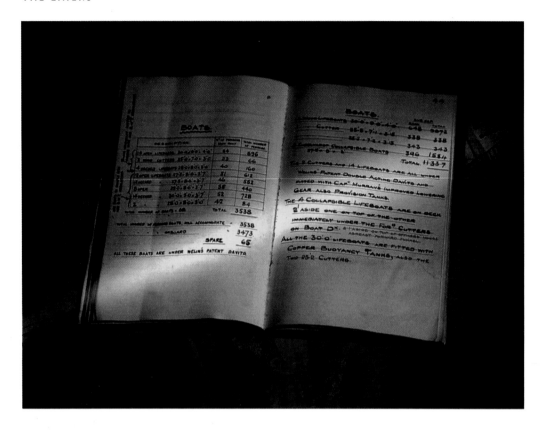

Olympic plans for *Titanic* were made in red. On one double-page, under the heading 'Boats', was a list of the boats planned for both giant liners. The left-hand page showed the breakdown of maximum crew and passenger numbers the ships could carry. On the right was a column indicating the total seating available in the lifeboats that the builders and designers were about to supply. The equation read:

Boats will accommodate – 3,538

Passengers & crew – 3,473

Spare – 65

Then, through these details and those on the opposite page nominating full details of the style and type of boat to be supplied, Thomas Andrews had drawn a thick red line. But why?

'In the original designs for the *Titanic* as well as the *Olympic*, there was provision made for enough lifeboats for all the passengers, the crew and then spare capacity. But this changed because the owner, the White Star Line, decided that the ship would look too top-heavy,' explains Tom McCluskie, Harland & Wolff's historian. He continues:

> White Star said that too many boats spoiled the line of the ship. So the owner changed the specification to the very minimum number of lifeboats required. The original design plan for both the *Olympic* and *Titanic* had many more lifeboats. But the owners said that they took away from the graceful lines of the ships. Lifeboats were seen in those days as a necessary evil. Owners didn't particularly like them because they spoiled the nice looks of a ship. The *Titanic* had a one-year guarantee from Harland & Wolff. Our engineers were lost to a man, the same as for the White Star engineers. They really committed suicide. They stayed in the engine-room to keep the lights, the power and the pumps running as long as they possibly could. After the sinking, Harland & Wolff made no statement. The ship didn't belong to us at that point. Harland & Wolff never said the ship was unsinkable. The owners said the ship was virtually unsinkable, but no one ever said it was unsinkable.

Shock waves travelled around the world when news of the sinking and the number of people lost was confirmed. There were few corners of the world that were not touched in some way by the tragedy. Monuments were erected in towns, cities and villages around the globe, in places as remote as Broken Hill in the Australian outback where the local musicians erected a statue as their special tribute to the musicians who continued to play as the giant liner sank.

If it could be said that any good came out of the *Titanic* sinking, it came in the aftermath of the tragedy when international rules for safety at sea where overhauled, amended and brought up to date with the technology of the time. Among these was a complete set of new regulations requiring every registered sea-going ship to carry enough lifeboat accommodation for everyone on board. The general public deserved and demanded to be reassured of the safety measures on board the ships on which they travelled.
However, the sinking of the *Titanic* was far more than just the loss of the largest ship in the world, and 1,503 unfortunate people. American author and historian Bill Miller states:

> Many people felt that the sinking of the *Titanic*, a mechanical marvel, unsinkable, going down on its maiden trip was actually the beginning of the end, the slow decline of the British Empire. Remember, Britain was at the forefront in 1912, so it was a very symbolic act beyond just the ship and White Star, and liners. It was kind of a political event, in a sense.

That sense of decline did not go unnoticed to Admiral Alfred von Tirpitz, in charge of the German naval build-up, and his counterpart in England, the young First Lord of the Admiralty, Winston Churchill. They were both increasing their battle fleets, spoiling for a conflict which, day by day, was becoming more imminent. Albert Ballin, Managing Director of the Hamburg-Amerika Line, had for years been trying to persuade Germany's leaders, including his friend the Kaiser, to halt the build-up of German naval forces. He wanted any contest between the two rival nations to 'not be between dreadnoughts, but between the *Aquitania*s of the Cunard Line and the *Vaterland*s of Hamburg-Amerika'.[7] Ballin had ordered three new ships to be larger and faster than the *Mauretania*, *Lusitania* and, later, the 45,600-ton *Aquitania*, launched from John Brown's Clydebank shipyard in April 1913. The contest he was looking forward to was a battle between the great commercial shipping lines for outright dominance of the North Atlantic passenger business.

But the Kaiser and his war advisers were formulating other, much more serious plans.

Ballin's trio was to consist of the *Imperator* at 52,117 tons, launched in May 1912, *Vaterland* at 54,282 tons, which went into service in 1914, and *Bismarck* at 56,551 tons, which was incomplete when the First World War broke out. Prior to the launching of *Imperator*, Cunard announced that the *Aquitania* would be 1ft (30cm) longer than the new German ship. Having billed their ship as 'the biggest ship in the world', it seemed that Hamburg-Amerika would be made to look silly if, in fact, her Cunard rival was larger. So Hamburg-Amerika ordered a large eagle-shaped figurehead to be added to the *Imperator*, increasing her overall length by some 10ft (3m) – making her exactly 9ft (2.7cm) longer than the Cunard ship.

Vaterland, the largest liner in service and the ultimate symbol of German industrial achievement, had left New York two days before when Austria-Hungary declared war on Serbia. Three days later, on 31 July 1914, she was ready to leave New York for Hamburg when word arrived that French

51

and British cruisers were waiting to seize her when she reached international waters. Her sailing was cancelled until further orders.

On 3 August Germany declared war on France and, the next day, Britain declared war on Germany. The western world was about to enter four years of carnage. For the ocean liners of all nations, it was the beginning of a new era. Many had been designed and built for fast conversion to armed cruisers, to transport troops or as hospital-ships. From symbols of proud nations they became prime targets. The liners were destined to play a major role in this terrible war.

At the beginning of hostilities, the British First Lord of the Admiralty, Winston Churchill, ordered his navy to blockade Germany. Within months, food prices soared; rationing was introduced and strictly enforced. In retaliation, the German High Command ordered its U-boats to attack British shipping, subject to the international rules of war. This required U-boat captains to stop and evacuate all persons on board a ship before they sank it. For a while the U-boat captains complied with this order. It was possible when the ships were small and unarmed but with larger, faster vessels, almost surely fitted with concealed heavy guns, the code of gentlemanly behaviour was soon ignored.

As war supplies and troops from the distant Commonwealth countries – Australia, New Zealand, Canada and South Africa – began to arrive in Britain on converted liners, the U-boat campaign became a vital element of the German war strategy. Like the British blockade of Germany, the U-boats wanted to prevent vital supplies getting through to Britain.

On 1 May 1915 Cunard's *Lusitania* sailed from New York bound for Liverpool. On board were almost 2,000 passengers and crew, including American citizens. The Americans belonged to a neutral country, and the liner was a ship of the British Cunard Line, flying the Union Jack. The day before her departure, the Imperial German Embassy in Washington had published a warning in New York newspapers that vessels flying the flag of Britain or her allies were subject to destruction, and that persons entering the war zone encompassing the British Isles did so at their own risk. This notice had been published next to the Cunard advertisement advising details of the *Lusitania*'s departure.

NOTICE!

TRAVELLERS intending to embark on the Atlantic voyage are reminded that a state of war exists between Germany and her allies and Great Britain and her allies; that the zone of war includes the waters adjacent to the British Isles; that, in accordance with formal notice given by the Imperial German Government, vessels flying the flag of Great Britain, or of any of her allies, are liable to destruction in those waters and that travellers sailing in the war zone on ships of Great Britain or her allies do so at their own risk.

IMPERIAL GERMAN EMBASSY

WASHINGTON, D. C., APRIL 22, 1915.

OPPOSITE:
Unfortunately top-heavy and largely unstable, the mighty *Imperator* is even seen listing slightly in this dramatic maiden voyage view.

ABOVE:
This advertisement appeared in the New York papers next to the Cunard notice advising sailing information for the *Lusitania*.

There were rumours that the ship was carrying illicit war materials in the guise of legitimate cargo. This was denied by Cunard, and the ship was cleared for departure by US port officials. So she sailed, on schedule, at 12.30pm, bound for Liverpool in England. It was generally believed that the *Lusitania* was beyond attack. She was considered too fast for German U-boats, and to have American citizens on board would surely guarantee the safety of the giant Cunard ship. Or so the world thought.

NOTES

1 Melvin Maddocks, *The Great Liners*, Time-Life Books, page 28.
2 Maddocks, *op. cit.* page 29.
3 Maddocks, *op. cit.* page 30.
4 James Duggan, *The Great Iron Ship*, Harper & Brothers, 1953, page 97.
5 Lord Kinross, *Between Two Seas*, John Murray, 1968, page 269.
6 Michael Moss and John Hume, *Shipbuilders to the World*, Blackstaff press, 1986, page 31.
7 Maddocks, *op. cit.* page 57.

BELOW:
Aquitania leaving the basin at the Clydebank shipyards in April 1913.

CHAPTER TWO

CALMS AND STORMS

On 7 May 1915, after an uneventful crossing, *Lusitania* was approaching the southern tip of Ireland, only a day's steaming from Liverpool. On the evening of 6 May the first of four warnings from the British Admiralty regarding U-boat activity in the area had been received. Extra lookouts had been posted, the ship's lifeboats uncovered and swung out on their davits but, contrary to all Admiralty instructions, *Lusitania* did not maintain maximum speed nor did she continue her zigzag course. Captain Turner instead slowed down his giant vessel to take a bearing off the Old Head of Kinsale on the southern Irish coast. It was around noon on a calm and sunny spring day.

THE WORLD AT WAR

The German U-boat U20, under the command of Lieutenant Walther Schwieger, had seen the approaching vessel, recognized her as British, dived and, at full speed, set a course to intercept and attack. Schwieger could hardly believe his eyes: a giant enemy ship, perfect visibility, smooth seas and the captain reducing speed. It was the situation that submarine commanders dream about. As *Lusitania* crossed his bows, Schwieger gave the order to fire. A single torpedo sped towards the liner. It struck just under the starboard bridge wing. A thick column of steam and water spouted nearly 200ft (60m) in the air, and with it went pieces of coal and wood and steel splinters. The *Lusitania* began to list almost immediately. Then there was a tremendous second

LEFT:
Lusitania memorial erected in the centre of Cobh, formerly Queenstown, the port in southern Ireland where many of those who died in the tragedy are buried.

OPPOSITE:
The sinking of the *Lusitania*, 7 May 1915, triggered a bitter propaganda campaign by the British against Germany. It was difficult for many to separate fact from fiction, as the media of the day depicted the horror of the sinking and the plight of its civilian passengers and crew. In this painting the artist has incorporated the medals struck by a German individual to celebrate the sinking. The medals were later copied and widely distributed in Britain.

blast that ripped apart the bow section. Many survivors maintained that it was neither a second torpedo nor even a boiler explosion, but instead illicit wartime cargo in the forward hold that caused the blast. The *Lusitania* sank within 18 minutes. The number of people who perished was 1,198, including 758 passengers. Among the dead were 128 Americans, including 35 children. Of all liner tragedies, the sinking of the *Lusitania* is surrounded by more controversy than any other vessel before or since.

The First World War was nine months old when this tragic sinking occurred and there was no secret at the time that German U-boats were forming a blockade around Britain, hunting down and sinking all ships carrying supplies to feed the British war machine, and yet shipping companies flying the Union Jack were still operating normal peacetime passenger schedules to and from the United States. The Cunard Line, with *Lusitania*, was one of these. Author John Maxtone-Graham:

> It looks so naive now that any shipping company could, in 1915, have continued to keep a vessel in service across the hostile North Atlantic when it was a German proclivity to sink anything

in sight. The *Lusitania* just steamed across. They painted the funnels black, they blacked out the ship, but they advertised the sailings and it was no secret to the Germans where the ship was, and of course, off the Old Head of Kinsale, in May, the end came. And that, in a sense, set the tone for the world: after almost 100 years of the Congress of Vienna until the sinking of the *Lusitania*, civilians were now not safe. There was no respect for civilian traffic as opposed to naval or war traffic.

Was *Lusitania* carrying war supplies, particularly explosives? Cunard denied it, and the New York authorities cleared the ship prior to her departure. The world knew that she had been designed and built for conversion to an armed cruiser, and with her peacetime red-coloured funnels blacked out, and rumours circulating that the British were using her to smuggle war supplies, there was little wonder the Germans were suspicious of her. Frank Braynard has no illusions about the sinking:

> I think that she was loaded with ammunition. She was a ship of war if any ship was. And we shouldn't scream, 'You bloody murderer', damning the Germans for sinking her. They were doing their best to blockade England, and this was one tragic way they had to make an effective blockade – sink anything that went nearby.

Would the U-boat captain Walther Schwieger have had any hesitation in firing that fatal torpedo at *Lusitania*? Not according to German naval historian, Dr Jürgen Rohwer, 'He had no doubt. He followed the regulations he had and attacked. There was no problem for him, I think.' And another German ocean-liner historian, Arnold Kludas, puts the latest theory of the sinking, after a detailed exploration of the sunken *Lusitania* by Robert Ballard, discoverer of the Titanic, into perspective:

> We know that the second explosion was not a cargo of ammunition as the Germans thought, and it was not a second torpedo as the British always thought, but it was the coal bunkers. There was some gas and dust in these near-empty bunkers and when the torpedo hit the liner, the carbon dust was ignited and the whole thing exploded. It was one of the first cases of modern, total war. A terrible thing, of course.

December 1899. Mounted troops of the Royal Australian Artillery unsaddling their horses on a wharf in Sydney. The steamship *SS Warrigal* is waiting to take them aboard for service in South Africa during the Boer War.

There were also accusations made in some areas that Winston Churchill, the First Lord of the British Admiralty, had set up the whole thing to bring the United States into the war. There is no direct evidence to support this theory although Churchill, in a top-secret letter written some months before the *Lusitania* sinking, wrote of the 'importance of attracting neutral shipping to British shores in the hope of enticing the US into the war with Germany'. He stressed Britain's need for ocean trade. 'The more the better,' he said, 'but if some of it gets into trouble, better still.'

In the port of Queenstown, now Cobh, the dead and the survivors were brought ashore. In a mass grave in the old cemetery in this historic Irish town many of the victims lie buried under a simple headstone, which reads: '*Lusitania*, 15 May 1915'. As the British and American nations mourned their dead, propaganda started. American opinion was very much split over their delayed entry into the war on the side of Britain. Their factories were doing good business providing the war supplies without putting US lives at risk. The large German population in the United States was certainly against supporting a war against its old homeland. Britain needed all the help she could muster and the *Lusitania* sinking was used to foster powerful anti-German feelings.

A German citizen produced around 200 medallions that lauded the sinking of the *Lusitania*. British propagandists obtained one, produced 250,000 copies and distributed them as a prime example of how Germany was celebrating the sinking. 'Actuality' newsreels were also screened in British cinemas purporting to show the sinking. Victims were depicted swimming to lifeboats as the giant Cunarder was sinking in the background. It was actually filmed in a duck-pond on Wimbledon Common, on the outskirts of London. Paid 'extras' were the 'passengers'; the ship was a three-ply wooden mock-up (badly out of proportion!), and the director choreographed the action to suit the cameras.

A leading animator in Britain produced an account of the sinking, which was widely screened throughout the UK. And, of course, the newspapers and the poster artists in both the United States and Britain had a field-day. But if this was a campaign designed to bring the United States into the war, it failed. It was two more years before continuing attacks by German U-boats on American shipping, and the announcement by Germany on 31 January 1917 of unrestricted submarine warfare, eventually pressured President Woodrow Wilson, on 6 April, to declare war on Germany.

When war broke out in 1914, a number of the major German liners happened to be in New York. The new *Vaterland*, the largest ship in the world and the absolute embodiment of Albert Ballin's dreams for domination of the North Atlantic by ships of his beloved Hamburg-Amerika Line, was waiting to depart for Hamburg. The voyage was cancelled for fear of an ambush by British and French cruisers once she reached international waters. For almost two years 'the greatest ship in the world' lay alongside a New York wharf. She was not officially interned, but tied up pending further sailing instructions.

It was the same situation with the *Amerika, George Washington, Kaiser Wilhelm II, Kronprinz Wilhelm* and *Kronprinzessin Cecilie* – 'the Fleet the Kaiser built us' as War Secretary Josephus Daniels dubbed this windfall of mighty passenger liners.[1] the great *Imperator* remained in Germany as did the partially completed third member of the Ballin trio, *Bismarck*. Once the United States declared war, all German ships in their ports were confiscated, reflagged and prepared for trooping duty. It was ironic that these peacetime liners would carry the American troops to fight against the German nation that had conceived and produced them. Of all the German ships, it was the *Vaterland,* renamed *Leviathan*, that caused the most damage to the German war effort, by transporting some 100,000 troops across the Atlantic. The use of *Vaterland* for war, the sight of *Imperator* tied up, going rusty, the unfinished *Bismarck* and the futility of the 'war to end all wars' caused Albert Ballin to take his own life only

The '*Lusitania* Medal', struck in Germany to celebrate the sinking of the *Lusitania*. Only a couple of hundred were ever minted. However, in Britain, 250,000 copies were distributed as an example of how Germans perceived the tragedy.

RIGHT:
1915: 3rd Australian General Hospital about to leave for service during the First World War aboard the troop transport ship *Mooltan*, bound for England then Lemnos.

BELOW:
Australians went to war as part of the Empire and are seen landing from a P&O steamer in 1916.

two days before the Armistice was signed. It seemed unlikely that there might be anyone left in an exhausted and disillusioned world who would dream again his dream.[2]

There was nothing new about peacetime liners being converted for war. It had happened in the Crimean War in 1850 when the *Great Britain* and a fleet of P&O and Cunard paddle-wheelers took French and British troops to war. In the Boer War of 1900 it was again commercial liners converted to troop-ships that brought the soldiers of the British Empire to South Africa to fight for 'Queen and Empire'.

The Union and the Castle Lines were amalgamated in February 1900 to form the famous Union Castle Line, a legendary communication link between 'Mother England' and its very rich South African colony. In the First World War, great convoys of liners once more carried the troops from British Commonwealth countries to foreign battlefields to fight for King and country. For young Australians and New Zealanders it was a chance in a lifetime to board ships they had only read about, bound for distant shores they had only dreamt of. It was a big adventure that would soon be over, then they would be home again, wiser, richer and full of the joys of overseas travel. So they marched up the gangplanks singing and whistling, embarking happily.

At the landing at Gallipoli in the Dardanelles, in 1915, the Turkish gunners were waiting on the cliff-tops as wave after wave of British, Australian and New Zealand troops landed on the beaches from anchored troop-ships. Among the fleet of vessels were ships of P&O, the Orient Line and the Union Castle Line. Two giant liners, *Mauretania* and *Olympic*, painted in battleship grey, were among the British ships. The failure of this major campaign, with enormous loss of life, embodied the grim reality of the war, a war that raged on land, sea and in the air for over four years and cost millions of lives.

In this conflict the liners played a significant, but changing role. The concept of turning 'superliners' into effective armed merchant cruisers capable of matching the naval vessels designed specifically for war was soon found wanting. The major problem was the amount of coal they consumed, and the limited amount they could carry. Designed as transatlantic 'greyhounds', they were indeed fast, but the whole economy of their operation was based on high speed sustained for four to five days. Then they went back into port to refuel and start again. War was different. The cruising range required was enormous and economical medium-speed cruising, with reserve for full power in short bursts, was outside their design characteristics. Although many were strengthened in the building process to take reasonably heavy guns, their hulls and superstructure were not capable of withstanding the rigours of war. Their manoeuvrability was also limited and a real drawback to their effectiveness in war.

Cunard's *Mauretania* and *Lusitania*, built with British government funding for fast conversion to armed merchant cruisers, never operated in this role. *Mauretania* was converted but never commissioned as an armed vessel. They could never have kept up her coal supplies! She became a highly successful troop-ship and hospital-ship, and worked almost non-stop at these duties for the duration of the war. *Lusitania* was never converted but retained by Cunard to operate the scheduled passenger service to New York. She did this until her sinking in May 1915. The *Aquitania*, together with two other Cunard ships, *Caronia* and *Carmania*, were also converted to armed cruisers. Because it had been proven unsuitable for the very large ships to operate as armed vessels, *Aquitania* was relegated to troop duties, later became a hospital-ship, and ended the war as one of the most famous of allied troop-ships.

At least six years before the war had begun, the captain of every German liner had carried a book of instructions on what course of action to take in the event of war. Supply-ships carrying guns, ammunition and provisions were operating in discreet ocean localities around the world, standing by to convert peacetime liners to wartime cruisers. Where the British had ports around the world where conversion of their liners could take place, Germany was less fortunate and had to make other arrangements. The instructions the captains carried were no secret, as German maritime author Arnold Kludas explains:

> When it came to war, they had sealed orders what to do, in the same style as it was with other nations. And in time of peace, the officers and the crew must have been instructed what to do in case of war. They got these instructions ten years before the war, but that's only natural, otherwise it's pretty senseless to convert to a merchant cruiser if nobody knows how to manage it and what to do then.

The great liners went to war: the beautiful *Mauretania* in dazzle-paint camouflage during the 1914–18 conflict.

Germany's early 'superliner', North German Lloyd's *Kaiser Wilhelm der Grosse*, launched in 1897, was an early victim. Converted to an armed cruiser, and painted grey and black, she sank a few small ships, intercepted two passenger liners loaded with women and children that she let go, and then was caught by an ageing British cruiser, *Highflyer*, while taking on coal off the African coast. After a short and bitter duel the *Kaiser Wilhelm der Grosse* rolled over and sank.

It was hard to believe the fierce rivalry between commercial shipping lines would ever escalate to actual armed combat between two liners, but on 14 September 1914 this occurred. Cunard's liner *Carmania*, converted to an armed cruiser, came across the Hamburg Sud-Amerika Line's new liner, *Cap Trafalgar*, which was refuelling off the Ilha da Trindade in the South Atlantic. The *Cap Trafalgar*, only commissioned in March that year, had rendezvoused with an old, armed Hamburg-Amerika Line gunboat after leaving Montevideo, had transferred heavy guns and ammunition, taken on supplies, removed her dummy third funnel and was about to begin operations as an armed cruiser. With only two funnels, it was hoped the deception would pass her off as a British Union Castle ship. In this guise she cruised the waters off the South American coast in search of British ships.

Off the Ilha da Trindade, on a pre-arranged schedule, two colliers were waiting to refuel the *Cap Trafalgar* when the *Carmania* arrived. As the colliers fled, the German liner faced the British liner. After a fierce battle lasting almost an hour, *Cap Trafalgar*'s engines stopped, and a short time later the German liner capsized and sank. Almost all the crew was picked up by one of the returning colliers.

While the *Olympic*, the first of the proposed White Star's trio of worldbeaters, and sister ship to the *Titanic*, worked ceaselessly during the entire war period as a troop-ship, the third and largest ship, *Britannic*, serving as a hospital-ship in the Aegean in 1916, hit a German mine and sank. Robert Ballard, the underwater explorer, describes the wreck of the *Britannic* as the most beautifully preserved liner of all those he has dived on.

There is little doubt that the sheer carrying capacity of peacetime liners converted for war has been instrumental in the extension of global warfare. The ability to move entire armies over vast ocean distances to fight on foreign battlefields has allowed military strategists to expand the very scope of their hostilities. As well as transporting troops to battle, liners converted to hospital-ships provided a sanctuary for the sick and wounded in the First World War – as they did as far back as the Crimean War when Florence Nightingale travelled to the battlefields in the converted P&O side-paddler *Vectis*.

Over 9 million tons of shipping were lost between 1914 and 1918, in a war that devastated the shipping lines of all nations and left the world with an immediate shortage of passenger liners. With the signing of the Armistice at 11am on the eleventh day of the eleventh month of 1918, it was not only Germany that had suffered in defeat. The nations of Europe, where the battles had raged for four years, were ravaged. So too was Britain, which was financially destitute and nationally exhausted. As the British liners limped back to the Commonwealth countries, taking home the sick, wounded and the troops, it was in fact the United States that emerged comparatively unscathed, and industrially and financially more powerful that ever before.

When the last shot of the war was fired and silence fell over the battle-scarred fields of France and Belgium, the ships of the world once more opened their blacked-out portholes and turned on the deck-lights. In all, 2,749 British ships were sunk, accounting for nearly 40 percent of their pre-war fleet. In addition, 14,287 merchant sailors, troops and civilians had lost their lives, mostly due to the relentless success of the German U-boat campaign.

The Cunard Line lost 22 ships, 56 percent of its total pre-war tonnage, with three of its associated companies, Anchor, Commonwealth & Dominion and Brocklebank, adding another 45 vessels to this one shipping conglomerate's losses. P&O and British India lost almost half their pre-war tonnage, and yet ended the war with a greater tonnage that their combined fleets had in 1914, a situation common throughout shipping circles, as explained by Tony Slaven, Professor of Economics and Social History at Glasgow University:

At the end of the war the expectancy was for full order books and for the shipbuilding industry to boom for a decade at least thereafter. But in the course of war, world shipbuilding capacity had about doubled, mainly because the United States, which had always built for its internal traffic on the lakes and rivers, built huge tonnage to meet the demands during the war. The world merchant marine, although it had lost 9 million tons, was much larger at the end of the war than it was before the war, and the world shipbuilding industry had doubled its annual output.

OPPOSITE:
Union Castle Line boasted of a 'mere seventeen days' between London and Capetown in those pre-airline days.

As the world cleaned up the wreckage and rubble, repaired and replaced all that had been broken and destroyed, and began a massive rebuilding campaign, the passenger lines took on the huge task of refurbishing their old ships, and trying to find the capital to build new ones.

On 28 June 1919, representatives of the warring nations met in Versailles, France, to sign a treaty designed to prevent such a war ever happening again. The League of Nations was formed, and territories surrendered by defeated Germany were divided up between the other nations of Europe. Under the Treaty of Versailles the victorious Allies arraigned the Kaiser, who had taken refuge in Holland. Then it was time to assess the amount Germany would have to pay in compensation, either in cash, or in kind. With the key ships in its fleet of passenger liners comparatively unscathed, these giant liners formed a major item on the list of the war reparations. The 'prize' vessels were allocated to the various victorious governments which, in turn, handed them to their own national shipping lines.

The *Imperator*, the 52,117-ton Hamburg-Amerika giant, which had been laid up in Hamburg for the duration of the war, was given to the Cunard Line. She was renamed *Berengaria* and became the flagship of the line. *Vaterland*, at 54,282 tons the largest passenger ship to enter service under the German flag, remained in the United States as the *Leviathan*. *Bismarck*, the largest of the Ballin trio at 56,551 tons, was handed to the British White Star Line to replace their *Britannic*. She had not been completed when war broke out and White Star commissioned Harland & Wolff to supervise completion of the vessel in Germany. She was renamed *Majestic*, and was at that time the largest passenger liner in the world. Another major vessel transferred to White Star under this reparation arrangement was the North German Lloyd's 34,350-ton *Columbus*. She was renamed *Homeric*.

Cunard alone placed orders for thirteen ships, at the time the largest commercial order, in terms of tonnage, ever placed. But these were not giant 'superliners' like the pre-war *Mauretania* and *Aquitania*. They were less than half the size, built to a budget and designed to fill an immediate need on the North Atlantic. This was the trend of the times adopted by all

To South Africa in Seventeen Days

UNION-CASTLE LINE

WEEKLY MAIL SERVICE.
Head Office. 3 Fenchurch Street. London. E.C.3.

the competing lines: smaller, cheaper-to-build liners that would maintain company services on the well-established, pre-war routes. In the case of Cunard and White Star, the *Aquitania, Mauretania* and the *Olympic*, once refurbished for peacetime duties, would become the big name ships of their fleets. Without opposition from German rivals, they would be supreme on the North Atlantic.

In 1921 the Union Castle Line, operating on the Southampton–South African ports route, launched their new liner, built by Harland & Wolff, and called *Arundel Castle*, a magnificent four-stacker. That same year, P&O placed orders for seven liners for their London–Bombay and London–Sydney services. One of these, the *Rawalpindi*, would feature in the next war, which erupted only two decades after the end of the First World War.

AMERICA THE GOLDEN

The last great wave of passengers, clamouring for berths on ships leaving England and Europe for the United States, Canada and for any other country that promised hope and freedom from persecution, were immigrants. In 1913, almost one and a half million people boarded ships bound for the United States. At the end of the war there were almost as many desperate people once again seeking passage out of Europe. For the vast majority, the open-door policy of the United States and the success stories filtering back attracted the homeless and destitute to this land of opportunity. In steerage class, in often appalling conditions, the short five to six-day voyage across the North Atlantic, whatever the weather, had to be more appealing that the prospect of thirty to forty days to, perhaps, Australia or New Zealand. The United States was by far the most popular destination for these people. The flood of migrants into the United States that had begun in the late 1800s, after four years' hiatus during the First World War, began again as soon as the liners were operating. Getting shipping services back to normal as fast as possible to capitalize on this enormous captive market of passengers was the main aim of every passenger company. The guaranteed profits from this trade alone would help make up for the lean years during the war.

Between 1892 and 1924, over 12 million immigrants arrived in New York alone and, almost without exception, each of them passed through the Ellis Island immigration reception centre. Only first- and second-class passengers were spared Ellis Island. Their status of travel alone qualified them for immediate acceptance as 'new' Americans. As the arriving liners came within sight of the Statue of Liberty, thousands of steerage passengers, getting their first glimpse of this great icon of freedom, liberty and hope, imagined it would be simply a matter of walking down the ship's gangplank to begin their new life. But there was one major clearance process they had to undergo before that last step, and that occurred on Ellis Island. First, the new arrivals underwent a preliminary medical check, which led to a more detailed examination if any physical defects or ailments were noticed. Any contagious disease meant automatic expulsion.

Next was an interview with an inspector which, in most cases, took place through an interpreter. In around two minutes, the inspector asked a number of fixed questions and made up his mind as to the suitability, or not, of a person to enter the United States. If there were any problems in the first interview, a second could follow 'some time later', when three inspectors would carry out further interrogation.

Once past this procedure, it was 'Welcome to America' and the papers were stamped accordingly; the immigrant became a 'new' American. If either the medical examination or the series of interviews resulted in rejection, it was back to the liner for the long, heartbreaking trip home. Quite often complete families, grandparents, parents and children arrived together and, through the process, some members were accepted while others were rejected. In many cases, as those accepted proceeded through one door and the other through a different, 'reject' door, it was the last time the family would be together. Usually it was the older members who failed and, for those, Ellis Island, instead of beginning a new life of hope became an isle of despair.

Ellis Island is preserved and restored today as a memorial to the millions who travelled by liners to begin a new life in the United States. Authors and film-makers George Perec and Robert Bober aptly describe Ellis Island as: '. . . a sort of factory for manufacturing Americans, a factory for transforming emigrants into immigrants; an American-style factory, as quick and efficient as a sausage factory in Chicago. You put an Irishman, a Ukraine Jew, or an Italian from Apulia into one end of the production line and at the other end – after vaccination, disinfection, and examination of the eyes and pockets – an American emerged.' Perec and Bober also present the other side of the Ellis Island story: 'No more than 2 percent of all emigrants were turned away from Ellis Island. That still amounts to 250,000 people. And between 1892 and 1924, there were 3,000 suicides on Ellis Island.'

For the shipping companies the immigrant trade was huge business that returned incredible profits, as author Frank Braynard explains, using his favourite ship as an example:

The *Vaterland* could carry 3,000 immigrants. The first-class passengers were the icing on the cake. They were the ones who

RIGHT:
Steerage dining areas were quite bare: exposed steel bulkheads, ceilings and floors, naked light bulbs, long benches rather than chairs, and rows of tables placed tightly together. This view is aboard the *Imperator* in 1913.

OPPOSITE:
Pre-war splendour: the First-Class Restaurant aboard the *France* of 1912 included a grand stairway as an entrance. It immediately proved to be a highly popular addition, especially with the well-dressed ladies, and was subsequently incorporated into all future French transatlantic liners.

had the most beautiful cabins. First class had two-thirds of the ship, but four-fifths of the people who went on the ships were crowded into one-fifth of the space as immigrants. They had to build ships big enough, bigger and bigger and bigger, to accommodate the immigrants. They paid for those great liners.

Robert Wall puts the role of the liners into perspective when he adds, '. . . without the big superliners there wouldn't have been any American dream'.

In 1924 the American immigration laws were changed, severely restricting immigration to the United States. The government used the census taken in 1910 as a base figure to calculate the number of future immigrants. The new number was calculated as a small percentage of each nation's US residents as at that date. Its immediate effect was reflected in the balance sheets of every shipping company operating passenger liners on the Atlantic run. Their biggest source of profits had all but disappeared overnight. But that was certainly not the only problem the lines faced in the years that followed the end of the First World War.

ON PLEASURE BENT

As the 'Roaring Twenties' went their way, and young flappers danced to the music of the era, the world economy was on a roller-coaster – it was booming at one moment and almost bust the next, as it tried to regain its equilibrium. In the immediate aftermath of the war, costs of building and operating ships had dramatically escalated. Although the shipbuilding yards were kept busy refurbishing the wartime fleets and meeting new orders, the numbers of people seeking jobs far exceeded the work available. High national unemployment was a major problem facing governments throughout Britain and Europe. With treasuries empty because of fighting the war there was little money available to support the burgeoning social needs of disenchanted populations. The unions were gaining strength and industrial relations issues becoming a dominant factor in all industries, particularly in the shipyards and on the waterfront. Professor Tony Slaven:

The war had escalated prices and wages quite dramatically, by perhaps three or four times. The main policy adopted by the government and by employers was to make themselves more competitive by cutting costs, and since in the building of a ship at least 60 to 70 percent of the cost is labour, the obvious way to cut costs was to cut wages. Productivity never seemed to be considered.

There was also prohibition, introduced throughout the United States on 16 January 1920. It created another problem in the role of many of the North Atlantic passenger liners operating at this time, as author and liner expert Bill Miller recounts:

> When America went dry in the Twenties that meant American liners could not offer one of the most wonderful aspects of an ocean voyage – the long bars, you know, that little nip in the morning and the little nip after lunch, and brandies and all that kind of stuff. So the foreign lines really were able to capitalize on this. When the Depression set in, the general trade fell tremendously. Cunard and the White Star Line were really desperate for passengers. They had to turn away from what once was the lucrative Atlantic trade to run booze cruises – $10 trips overnight where you left New York City docks at 5pm, sailed outside the three-mile limit, on board say, *Mauretania* or *Majestic*. They'd open up the bars and Americans could drink themselves into oblivion until 8 o'clock the next morning, come back, and go ashore, and it all worked beautifully. So that was the alternative to prohibition. Those little mini-cruises, those $10 a night trips in the Twenties and Thirties were the first real effort to bring the masses to cruising. Because before that, cruising was strictly the domain of the rich and titled. So those booze cruises, one-nighters led to three-nighters, led to five-nighters, led to seven- and ten-nighters, and it just grew. That was the beginning of cruising for the masses as we know it today.

This use of ocean liners for the more leisurely purposes of pure passenger indulgence rather than transport, in voyages to 'nowhere', also saw the introduction of a single-class fare structure for the first time. This was a radical and bold experiment that mirrored the social changes and attitudes that were sweeping the world in the 1920s.

The 1920s also saw a major change in engine technology in the great liners. Oil was introduced to fire the furnaces,

replacing the filthy black coal that had fuelled the Industrial Revolution and steamships for over a century. Major new vessels would all be oil-fired; the older 'superliners,' including *Mauretania, Aquitania, Majestic* and *Vaterland*, were all converted to oil and, overnight, the showers of black soot that had plagued passengers and crew alike, it seemed forever, were no more. The smoke remained, but the soot had gone. Oil was not only cheaper and cleaner than coal, but the turnaround time and the labour costs of refuelling fell dramatically. It was the perfect fuel, or it appeared so until the oil crisis of the 1970s.

The immediate post-war period for the French Compagnie Générale Transatlantique, always known as the French Line, saw a new and dynamic Director, John Henri Dal Piaz, take over control of the organization. He was a visionary who reshaped the line's entire operation. Their old flagship, the *France*, commissioned in 1912, had created an enormous impact from the moment she went into service, providing a very 'French' alternative in style to all other vessels afloat. At 23,750 tons she was tiny compared with Cunard's *Mauretania* and *Lusitania* or Hamburg-Amerika's *Imperator* and *Vaterland*. But how strikingly different she was. Powered by four screws driven by a Parsons-designed turbine, *France* had twin funnels rather than the four that were the fashion at the time. And she was sleek, and her interior design and fittings created a floating Paris on the high seas, with brilliant technical innovations for passengers such as electric hair-curlers for the ladies and lifts (the first afloat) or, for those who preferred to make the grand entrance, a three-deck staircase complete with a bronze filigree banister. Fortunately, the *France* survived the war in which she had operated as an Allied armed cruiser, hospital-ship and transport for troops.

Dal Piaz had great hopes that ships of his line would rival those of Britain and Germany, when France re-emerged from the traumas of war, as it certainly would. He ordered completion of the *Paris*, a 34,500-tonner, which was partially completed when the war broke out, and a new, smaller ship, the *De Grasse*. With the old *France* completely renovated, and the two new liners, the French Line had three very distinctive vessels operating on the Atlantic by 1924. It was the beginning of a new maritime era for France, but this trio were little more than a mere 'entrée' for what was soon to follow.

The Twenties saw the end of the steerage class on most vessels, these cheaper berths being renamed 'tourist class'. It seemed that the term 'steerage' remained firmly associated with the immigrant trade in most people's minds, and as that trade had now markedly decreased, the shipping lines had to find another target group to fill their ships. They found the answer in the emerging middle class, and the young professionals in all types of vocations. Young American teachers were a particular target group to which the new tourist class appealed. They had money to spend, long vacation periods to fill, and the opportunity of travelling to Britain and Europe in the footsteps of their soldier brothers and fathers attracted these new travellers. For the first time it was not only the very rich or the very poor seeking a new life who filled the liners on the Atlantic run, but middle-aged and young people who were discovering the delights of international travel, and how easy, pleasant and affordable it was.

For the very rich, the shipping lines were creating accommodation and lifestyle experiences on board to rival anything available ashore. There were the greatest bands and entertainers available; food prepared by some of the world's most famous chefs, to be washed down with vintage wines; and suites and state-rooms that outclassed the finest hotels, all equipped with the latest comforts of the new age of technology. There were ballrooms to dance in, bars to relax at, decks to play on, gymnasiums to exercise in. There was nothing ashore really to compare with the luxuries available on an ocean liner, if money was unlimited. And for many, that was exactly the case. With the post-war blues to contend with, and wallets bulging, the liners were fast becoming moving hotels for the international social set as they voyaged the oceans to attend one cocktail party after another in the most exotic cities of the world. Even more exclusive were the super-expensive world cruises the lines 'invented'. In January 1922, for example, Cunard's luxuriously appointed *Laconia* sailed from New York on a 22-week, no-expenses-spared cruise. On board were 300 or so millionaires, most travelling with their own personal servants and all with more luggage and clothes than most people would dream of owning in an entire lifetime.

The majority of observers could not have guessed just how quickly the Germans would rejoin the ocean liner business after losing the 'war to end all wars'. They had been stripped completely of all their best passenger ships in the post-war reparations arrangements. But, in 1924, North German Lloyd's new flagship, the impressive, 32,300-ton *Columbus* made her maiden voyage from Bremerhaven to New York. It was the beginning of the re-emergence of the German lines on to the North Atlantic run. (There were, in fact, two North German Lloyd liners with the name *Columbus*. One was the 34,500-ton *Columbus*, which was launched in 1913 and given to the Allies as part of the war reparations – she began her working life as White Star Line's *Homeric*. The other ship, also laid down before the war, but not included in the reparations arrangements, was to have been named *Hindenburg*, but was launched in 1922 as North German Lloyd's *Columbus*.)

The major contestants for commercial travel on the North Atlantic were once again lining up, with new ships and post-war passion for a peacetime contest that, had he lived, Hamburg-Amerika's Albert Ballin would have thoroughly savoured!

BOOMS AND SLUMPS

The first 'superliner' built after the First World War was the illustrious 43,000-ton *Ile de France*, launched in 1926. The *Ile*, as she was fondly called, was the forerunner of a new generation of superships, the 'ships of state'. This new French ship was not, however, intended to be the largest or the fastest, or statistically superlative, in any way. Her appearance, while fashioned after the earlier *Paris* and other three-stackers, was not especially modern. It was based on a prescribed formula: two tall masts and three funnels. The great excitement about the *Ile* was concentrated on her

The 32,300 ton *Columbus*, completed in 1923, was Germany's first post-war liner. Later in life, she was given shorter funnels so as to further resemble even bigger German liners, the *Bremen* and *Europa*.

The *Ile de France* was perhaps the most spectacular and innovative liner of the 1920s – she began Art Deco styling at sea. She created 'ocean liner style' and soon shoreside designs were copying the ships. Previously it had been the reverse.

interior decoration. There had never been a liner quite like her. Earlier shipboard decor copied shore styles: castles, palaces and manor-houses, as well as dabbling in the exotic with Arabian, Egyptian, Moorish and even Moroccan concoctions. The basic intention behind such decor was to remind passengers of life on shore, even when they were coping with a rolling ship or a violent storm. The *Ile* represented a new age: she was an individual, a revolutionary, a forerunner, a trendsetter of her time. She inaugurated so-called 'ocean-liner style', early Art Deco on the high seas. Stephen Lash, the former President of the Ocean Liner Museum in New York, called the style, 'Early Ginger Rogers. It was floating Hollywood. Her interior did not copy any land establishment or hotel-like setting, but was a floating luxury resort unto itself. Soon, shoreside decorators would copy the ships, especially ones like the *Ile de France.*'

Her creation, largely underwritten by the French government, which wanted another floating embodiment of France to emulate the success of the highly acclaimed *France*

of 1912, took place at the Penhoet shipyards at Saint-Nazaire. Great excitement prevailed, not only at the yard, but throughout the country itself, as the hull of the giant vessel took shape. In June 1927, while being readied for her maiden trip across to New York, she was opened for the first time to a curious public – and quickly received rave reviews. She was everything that the lavish preliminary brochures and publicity sheets had promised.

The 390 first-class cabins were in many different styles. Her public rooms were as exciting as they were spacious. She introduced a new age in liner design, an era of angular and steel-tubed furniture, sweeping columns and lacquered panels, glossy floors, indirect lighting and such special distinctions as the longest bar then afloat. The first-class restaurant, missing the customary wood carvings and gilded eagles, was almost severe in its modernity, rose three decks in height and was compared to a modern-day Greek temple. The main foyer was four decks in height and the Gothic chapel had no less than fourteen pillars. Every amenity and convenience seemed to be aboard – even a merry-go-round for the youngest guests.

The berthing was arranged for three classes: first, cabin and an upgraded, improved third. Steerage had virtually disappeared by this time. Consequently, almost all Atlantic liner companies were forced to create far more comfortable third-class quarters which catered for budget tourists, teachers and students. But first class on the *Ile* was acclaimed the finest afloat. She had, for example, the greatest number of de luxe suites and cabins. By 1935, she had carried more first-class travellers than any other liner afloat. She was described by legions of voyagers as 'the cheeriest way to cross the North Atlantic' and as the ship that, more than any other, put the 'bon' in 'bon voyage'! Frank Braynard was among her greatest admirers:

> No ship ever had a reputation for glamour more remembered or better deserved than the *Ile de France*. One of my favourite ship folders, which came out in 1927, has heavy gold-coloured front and back covers. An illustration that sets the tone for this priceless, old brochure is a water colour depicting an elegant woman walking just below the ship's three huge, red and black funnels and holding her Great Dane on a leash. Even the great *Normandie*, which came along eight years later, did not make any greater splash than did the *Ile de France*.

The 1,786-passenger *Ile de France* was the first of a new breed of larger, more decoratively stunning Atlantic liners. She was so 'French', so brilliantly innovative in the Gallic manner that she even carried a small plane on board that could be launched while the ship was 200 miles or so from port. In the race by liners to be fastest to deliver the mail, the *Ile* had beaten all her rivals as the bags of mail she carried were landed ashore while the ship was still at sea.

On 29 October 1929, the Wall Street stock-market crash echoed around the world and plunged it into the worst Depression in history. Fortunes were lost in seconds; banks and other financial institutions became bankrupt; and the greatest unemployment in modern times ate deep into the heart of the democratic nations. The very fibre of traditional social and political systems was challenged as unemployed, homeless and hungry adults searched desperately for money and food for their families, and felt that they had lost their dignity and the right to work. It was a period in history when for many people a new bunch of 'isms' appeared to be the answer: Communism, Socialism and Fascism. Ironically, it was in the period of the great Depression that some of the world's greatest liners were conceived, built and operated.

During the 1920s Adolph Hitler and his National Socialist German Worker's Party were coming to the fore in German political circles, and in Italy, Benito Mussolini was leading his Fascist Blackshirts on a terror campaign against all those who opposed their views. In this volatile environment, liners operating on the UK/Europe route to the East, to India, the Far East, Australia and New Zealand via the Suez Canal were experiencing the last peacetime decade of the mighty British colonial Empire. In the film *Passage to India*, based on E. M. Forster's classic novel, the opening scenes take place in the palatial P&O passenger booking offices in London. A very formally dressed ticket agent prepares the tickets for the journey, from London to Bombay, for a young English girl named Adela Quested. She will be sailing on one of the great colonial liners of the 1920s, P&O's *Rawalpindi*. She is travelling to India to visit her English fiancé, who is city magistrate in Chandrapore. Accompanied by her mother, Mrs Moore, together they set off from the rain-splashed London docks in 1928.

It is a scene that was so typical of the era. After the disruptions of the First World War, colonial passenger services grew, prospered and produced a new generation of fine ships. Well removed from the more prestigious North Atlantic, these were often called the 'blue-water' liners. Instead of one-week crossings between UK/Europe and from New York, their voyages took four, six or eight weeks to Dar es Salaam and Lagos, Calcutta and Penang, Hong Kong and Sydney. They belonged to the likes of the legendary P&O Company, the British India Steam Navigation Company Limited, the Union-Castle Mail Line, the Orient Line, New Zealand Shipping Company, and then the more exotically titled Messageries

OPPOSITE:
P&O's 19,500-ton *Viceroy of India*, built for the Bombay service. She represented new standards of luxury and speed power by turbo-electric motors. This lovely liner was sunk by a German submarine in 1942.

Maritimes, Chargeurs Réunis, Rotterdam Lloyd, Nederland Royal Mail Line, Compagnie Maritime Belge and Lloyd Triestino.

The ambience and style of this era, the twilight time, in fact, of the huge colonial fleets, is perhaps best exemplified in Charles Owen's *Independent Traveller* (Routledge & Kegan Paul, 1966), which chronicles a homeward passage in P&O's noted *Viceroy of India*, sailing from Bombay via Aden, Suez, Marseilles and Gibraltar.

> Experienced travellers to the East preferred her [the *Viceroy of India*] to even newer vessels entering the famous service connecting Britain, through Suez, with India and the Far East. The passenger list [415 in first class and 258 second class] was headed by a majestic Commander-in-Chief, accompanied by mountains of baggage, a wife and an ADC. After lunch, I repaired to the lounge for coffee, choosing a pleasant table in the corner. Immediately, anxious stewards came whispering to me: if I did not mind, could I possibly sit elsewhere . . . this was His Excellency's favourite table. They were sure I would understand. Every first class passenger was pampered and had his ego stimulated to a gratifying degree . . . Everywhere servants waited to dance attendance on him – to bring him drinks, a quoit, a ping pong ball, a paper hat; to point the way to the cinema, the gymnasium, the swimming pool. Repeatedly, through the leisurely course of every day and night, an orchestra – sweating politely under the punkah-louvres – would take up its station in the palm-treed lounge, playing music to suit the moment. The grand climax in the small hours was a whirling series of old-fashioned waltzes, a gallop and finally, lights dimmed . . . that last exercise for flagging violins, 'Good Night Sweetheart'. Then the company would brace itself into immobility as the loyal strains of 'God Save the King' floated out through the opened windows, across the moonlit decks and away into the tropical night.

P&O was to the areas 'east of the Suez' what Cunard was to the Atlantic. Their first big, new ships after the First World War were two sisters, the *Maloja* and *Mooltan*, built for the UK–Australia passage, and a splendid quartet for the express run between London and Bombay, evocatively named the *Ranchi, Ranpura, Rawalpindi* and *Rajputana*. P&O also had

a small fleet of austere steamers such as the *Ballarat* and *Bendigo*, which each carried up to 2,500 immigrants in steerage-class conditions on the long-haul journey to Melbourne and Sydney. The larger *Viceroy of India* was the company's last traditional liner, completed in early 1929. 'If there was one ship I would like to go back and be captain of, it would have been the *Viceroy of India*. Everybody speaks so very, very highly of her,' says Commodore Ian Gibb, present-day master of P&O's new cruise-liner, the 70,000-ton *Oriana*. 'To have been in command of the *Viceroy of India* must have been the epitome of any P&O officer's career. She was the perfect ship back then.'

Sir John Cotten, who travelled with P&O in the 1920s and 1930s, recalls:

> P&O had the monopoly of the passenger traffic, especially to and from India, servicing the people, the Army and the business people in the large centres like Bombay, Calcutta and Madras. It was still the jewel in the crown in those days. The routes travelled by the P&O were all important to the British Empire. They transported the cargo and carried the soldiers. P&O carried the servants of the Crown. And, of course, it really wasn't just India. It was beyond to Malaya, Singapore, Australia and round the corner going up to Japan, Hong Kong and China. P&O was an all-purpose line. They were also the mail line. They maintained a very high standard of efficiency. P&O officers regarded themselves, so I'm told, as being on a par, if not superior in quality, to their counterparts in the Royal Navy. Yes, they provided a wonderful service.

John Havers, a retired purser on the Union Castle liners, recounts:

> You met all sorts of people on the colonial passenger ships in those days. We had a religious leader go from Port Sudan to Port Suez. He had come down on King Farouk's yacht. He said, 'It rolled about terribly. But your ship is so nice and steady.' And then there was another religious leader who asked to be shown around the ship. So I took him round and, of course the ship was full of Sudanese working the cargo. When they saw him, they all prostrated themselves completely on the floor, head down on the floor and stretched right out. I found this rather disconcerting.

RIGHT:
The first indoor swimming pool for P&O on board the opulent *Viceroy of India*.

FAR RIGHT:
Arrival in port – colonial style!

Havre docks warehouse. 'That decor was evocative of your destination, the exotic, mysterious Orient. The passengers who used it were mostly colonial administrators, and rich merchants and tea planters and so forth. And then coming home, it was the last link, a bridge of sorts, to what you were leaving behind. So it was all destination and ethnically connected.'

The glories of Holland, a great maritime and colonial power, were well incorporated into the decoration of the sister ships *Johan van Oldenbarnevelt* and *Marnix van St Aldegonde*, the Dutch flagships of the Amsterdam–Batavia trade. The style of a Belgian château featured aboard the

RIGHT:
The first indoor swimming pool for P&O on board the opulent *Viceroy of India*.

FAR RIGHT:
Arrival in port – colonial style!

You'd go round and people were prostrating themselves. He was used to it, of course, but I wasn't. It was quite amazing. A lot of work had to be done with the cargo and suddenly everyone dropped everything and laid down on the floor. These were the little things you got used to on the colonial runs.

'On the French ships going out to colonial Indo-China, you had Eastern decor,' said Jean-Paul Herbert, archivist of the Compagnie Générale Transatlantique and the Messageries Maritimes collections currently catalogued and stored in a Le

Leopoldville on the Congo trade route, and rich wood panelling was used aboard Portugal's *Nyassa*, which sailed to East and West African outposts.

In the mid-1920s with national governments financially drained, and shipping lines heavily committed to raising finance from the private sector for new ships, the decision by North German Lloyd to build two new, 50,000-ton ships came as a shock to the international shipping world. Their names would be *Bremen* and *Europa*. They would be two 'superships', out to capture the Blue Riband, and to re-establish German dominance of the North Atlantic.

'*Bremen* and *Europa* were financed by American money given to Germany as part of the "let's help Germany after the First World War" complex,' says Frank Braynard. Arnold Kludas explains that this money came largely from American payments the US government had made to the German government as compensation for the liners they had confiscated during the war. It was largely this finance that was used to underwrite the building costs of *Bremen* and *Europa*.

North German Lloyd's plans were to run a three-liner, weekly service using the two new ships, plus the smaller

The Main Lounge aboard the *Bremen* glittered – a feeling of the fresh and new, but with an ambience of comfort and relaxation. By day, the use of the tall windows created a fine balance between natural and artificial illumination. Overall, the room had the feel of some grand hotel in Berlin of the late '20s.

Columbus. The *Bremen* and *Europa* would be 'at least' 50,000 tons – not quite the very largest vessels afloat, but within their hulls would be the most powerful steam-turbine machinery to date. These would be the new German 'monsters', fitting successors to the turn-of-the-century four-stackers that established Germany as a dominant power on the North Atlantic early in the century. Unquestionably, these two new ships were also to show the world that Germany was successful again, and that the Blue Riband, held by Cunard's *Mauretania* for so long, would soon be under real threat from two new North German Lloyd 'greyhounds'.

Bremen was built, appropriately, in Bremen, and *Europa* in Hamburg. The two ships were launched on successive days in August 1928. And what radical vessels they were. Their hulls were long, rather low and certainly sleek. Both had rounded stems for increased speed and efficiency and, below the waterline, both liners had a bulbous bow, a unique design feature that, among other benefits, greatly reduced drag at sea. Overall, the ships were very much in the 1920s modern style with two tall masts and a pair of exceptionally low, squat funnels which were, in fact, raised within a year or so because of smoke and soot problems on the aft passenger decks.

It had been planned that *Europa* would be the first of the pair to go into service, but this was considerably delayed after a serious fire almost destroyed her in the Hamburg docks where she was built. Initial estimates suggested scrapping the 936-ft (280-m) long ship. But her North German Lloyd owners agreed to repairs, which lasted another year. The *Bremen* was delivered on schedule and entered service in July 1929. On her maiden voyage to New York, this latest German 'greyhound' lived up to her owners' expectations when she

LEFT:
It is August 1928 and the official launching of North German Lloyd's 938ft-long *Bremen* is just days away.

OPPOSITE:
In 1931, Canadian Pacific commissioned their *Empress of Britain*, the finest and fastest liner ever on the Atlantic service to St Lawrence.

shattered the record held by the *Mauretania*, creating a new average record speed for the crossing of 27.83 knots. The Blue Riband was back in German hands once more.

In March 1930 the *Europa*, finished at last, made her bid for a place in the record books. She took *Bremen*'s record for the westbound crossing, but could never beat her running mate's time for the eastbound journey. By 1933, the *Bremen* would hold both records to become the unchallenged Blue Riband champion of the North Atlantic.

In the spring of 1931 the ultra-luxurious, 42,300-ton *Empress of Britain*, the new flagship of the Canadian Pacific Line, and by far the largest and grandest liner ever built for the North Atlantic service to Canada, went into service. She was one of the great 'dream boats', big, glorious-looking, almost overpowering and unquestionably luxurious. She was specifically intended to lure transatlantic passengers to the St Lawrence route, to and from Quebec City. The plan was for *Empress of Britain* to provide a novel alternative service, not only to Canadians but also to American passengers from the Midwest. However, most US travellers continued to prefer the route through to New York. Consequently, the 1,195-passenger ship was not quite as successful as was hoped for.

Her disappointing appeal to passengers certainly had nothing to do with the ship itself. Her interiors were among the most lavish of their day. The Salle Jacques Cartier, the stunning first-class restaurant, was finished in natural oak and ranked as the largest unpillared room at sea. Two private dining-rooms, the Salle Montcalm and Salle Wolfe, were adjacent. The 165-ft (49.5-m) long Mall connected the ship's main public rooms and salons. The Knickerbocker Bar was cleverly decorated with humorous artwork depicting the evolution of the cocktail. Even the indoor pool was noteworthy: it had an illuminated glass ceiling, blue-coloured pillars and large, mounted turtles that spouted seawater into the pool itself.

The big *Empress* had another novelty about her: she was the first big Atlantic liner designed purposely with off-season, winter cruising in mind. Each winter, she was sent on a long, leisurely trip around the world. Lasting 125 days or so, she departed New York after Christmas and returned in spring.

ABOVE:
The *Rex*, Italy's premier luxury liner in the 1930s, was dubbed 'the Riviera afloat'. She had vast outdoor spaces, tiled pools and even real sand was scattered around her lido areas.

OPPOSITE:
The Italians were the so-called 'pioneers' of vast lido decks, large pools and attendants dressed in Venetian striped shirts. The *Conte di Savoia* was one of Italy's finest showcases for the Italian way of life.

Her route was rather traditional: across to the Mediterranean, North Africa and the Holy Land, through the Suez Canal and into the Red Sea, then to India, Ceylon, Southeast Asia and the Dutch East Indies, next upwards to China, Hong Kong and Japan, then across to Hawaii and California, and finally through the Panama Canal and back to New York. But while the *Empress of Britain* brought prestige to Britain and Canada, and status to Canadian Pacific, even her cruises lost money. The Depression greatly reduced her passenger loads. Sadly, she was one of the least profitable liners of the 1930s.

The first Italian 'superships', a pair of sister ships that catapulted Italy into transatlantic prominence, were completed under the personal eye of Benito Mussolini, the Fascist dictator who had gained control of the Italian parliament earlier in the decade. The two liners, *Rex* and *Conte di Savoia,* went into service just two months apart in 1932. Both were expected to be champion ships. In fact, only the first of them, the 51,000-ton *Rex*, succeeded. For two years, between 1933 and 1935, she held the Blue Riband, the only liner ever to do so under the Italian flag. But

otherwise, she and the 48,500-ton *Conte di Savoia* often sailed only half-full. It seems that the world's greatest liners appeared in a period of economic decline.

The *Rex* and the *Conte di Savoia* were quite different from one another. The former, for example, was the larger and the faster while the latter looked better and had superior fittings. Originally ordered for separate Italian owners, Italy's transatlantic shipping lines were merged under Mussolini's orders to eliminate unnecessary competition, to cut costs, and to show the world that Italy could design and build ocean liners equal to or better than any other maritime nation. Like all the other major maritime nations, liners were Italy's symbols of technological achievement – a bold peacetime statement of a nation's industrial capabilities. Mussolini saw *Rex* and *Conte di Savoia* as yet another important step in Italy becoming accepted as a major power.

These two Italian liners, which became known as 'Mussolini's Greyhounds of the Atlantic', introduced a new era in Atlantic passenger service: 'superliners' in the Mediterranean. The newly created Italian Line mounted a huge and enthusiastic campaign. 'The Riviera comes to meet you on board the *Rex* and *Conte di Savoia*.' Vast lido decks highlighted both ships and included reclining deck chairs, coloured umbrellas, stripe-shirted stewards, several tiled pools, and even real sand scattered about. Indeed, they were the first 'floating resorts' in this sense.

Teething problems plagued both these ships, however. In September 1932, and while still within Mediterranean waters on the start of her maiden voyage, the 879ft (263m)-long *Rex*'s engines failed. The Italians were embarrassed. The ship had to wait three days at Gibraltar for repairs while many of her anxious passengers grew impatient. New York City's Mayor, James J. Walker, fled to Cherbourg and caught the more punctual *Europa*. The Italians had actually hoped that the *Rex* would capture the Blue Riband on her maiden westbound crossing, but it took almost a year – not until August 1933 – before she took it from Germany's *Bremen* with a passage of 4 days, 13 hours.

The *Conte di Savoia* entered service two months after the *Rex*, in November 1932. All seemed to go well for her until, when 900 miles west of the American mainland, an outlet valve below the waterline jammed and blew a worrying hole in the ship's hull. In a matter of minutes seawater began to fill the ship's dynamo compartment. At first, it was kept secret from the passengers. The situation was, however, quite serious: initial inspections revealed that the 814ft (244m) liner might actually sink within as little as five hours. But the ship's engineers were very resourceful and one member of the crew went below and, in great danger, filled the hole with cement. The new ship was then safe and able to continue to New York.

The *Conte di Savoia* had another distinction. Like the *Olympic* and the *Titanic*, her owners thought the first ship in service might be overshadowed by the liner that followed. The *Rex*, they reasoned, needed a separate identity, her own claim to fame. So the *Conte di Savoia* became the 'roll-less ship'. She was the first major liner to have a gyro-stabilizer system, a system that predated modern fin stabilizers. It was said that the ship offered 'the smoothest sail on the Atlantic'. But, in reality, it was a rather limited system. It could only be used, for example, on westbound passages because of prevailing winds. And although it did help overcome the rolling motion, it had absolutely no effect on the pitching movement of the ship in a seaway. Many of her passengers were often surprised to find the *Conte di Savoia* rolling and pitching like other ships.

With the French, Germans and Italians all building new 'superliners', the British lines, and particularly Cunard, were still operating their pre-war 'monsters'. But that was all to change dramatically. As early as the mid-1920s Cunard were well advanced with their plans to retire the *Aquitania, Mauretania* and *Berengaria*. With these three ageing veterans, the British line had ruled the Atlantic for almost three decades, but with the French, and now the German liners, back in full force and holding the Blue Riband, it was time for Cunard to act. In 1926 their management and in-house design team had decided that two new giants would give them the capacity to run weekly crossings of the Atlantic, carrying the mail and the huge number of passengers required to return a profit to the shareholders. It was a simple equation: two very big ships would be more economical to run than three smaller vessels. The only real problem that faced

Cunard was the immediate finance to commission the first of the two new ships. They went to their old shipyard on the Clydebank, John Brown's, where the *Lusitania*, *Aquitania* and a host of smaller ships had been built, struck a deal, and, in December 1930, the keel of ship No. 534, the new giant Cunarder that would one day be named *Queen Mary*, was laid.

For four years the plans for the new ship were under constant development by the John Brown design team, which included a young Glasgow-trained naval architect who had joined the firm in 1924. (Although his name was John Brown, he had no family connection with his employers.) Still very much alive, and living not far from the yards where he spent his entire working life, from a youngster in the drawing-room to Managing Director of the entire establishment, John recalled for our cameras those days when he was part of history in the making:

> The Chairman of Cunard at the time was adamant there was no notion about building either the biggest or the fastest ship. All he wanted was a ship that would satisfy the requirement for a two-ship service between Southampton and New York. He quite frequently made this point, but the design led to a bigger ship and a faster ship.

At the same time as the John Brown team were designing '534', the *Queen Mary*, for Cunard, across the English Channel the French had plans for a ship that would arguably become 'the finest liner ever built'. She would be called the *Normandie*. In the shipyards at Saint-Nazaire, where the *Ile de France, France* and *Paris* had all been built before her, the French Line's new 'monster' was almost the same size as the proposed Cunard ship, although in many ways she was quite different. Russian émigré Vladimir Yourkevitch was in charge of designing the hull, and a large proportion of the finance was provided by the French government. With two German ships dominating the Atlantic, the French Line and the French government decided it was time for France to show the world it had a place to claim in maritime history.

Both Cunard and the French Line had knowledge of each others' plans to build a 'monster' liner. But neither knew exactly what the other was doing at any stage during the long building process. The two ships would be different – but how

different? They would be about the same size, but which would be the largest and, eventually, the fastest? As the world economies slipped slowly but surely towards the worst financial Depression ever experienced, these questions remained unanswered. John Brown recalls:

> We tested several hundred models before she was finally built, always refining it. The French *Normandie* was ahead of us a little bit. They had a naval architect of Russian origin called Yourkevitch, and he was making a great play about the 'Yourkevitch form' which, to some extent, was a refinement of the bow lines. We knew something of what he was doing, but of course we couldn't see his plans. But we were working on something similar, and in fact, in the long run, we had the advantage over him, but we did, as I say, several hundred models refining the form.

When asked if there had been any attempts at industrial sabotage during this highly competitive and confidential planning stage, John Brown was unhesitant in his reply:

> There wasn't a hope of it. As I told you, I was locked away in a back room along with another chap on the original development of the plans. And we certainly didn't get, or attempt to get, anything of the French plans. All we knew was that Yourkevitch was publicizing his own ideas, but no more than that.

With the recession biting deep into the British economy, in December 1931, Cunard were forced to stop work on '534'. The yard and the huge workforce on the Clydebank were devastated but, without sufficient funds to continue, Cunard was forced to make this tragic decision. In the yards at Saint-Nazaire, the French shipbuilders were more fortunate. The government funding continued and work on the *Normandie* carried on.

Between December 1931, and resumption of work in April 1934, the giant hull, No. 534, dominated the stark and silent shipbuilding yards along the Clydebank. If ever there was a symbol of the deepest days of the Depression, it surely was the unfinished rusting hull of '534' as it cast a shadow over the homes of tens of thousands of out-of-work people whose livelihood depended on the building of ships like this great Cunarder.

OPPOSITE:
Some 200,000 people were on hand to watch the *Normandie* being launched. The ways had been specially greased with 43 tons of soap and 2 tons of lard. The date was 29 October 1932.

78

RULE, BRITANNIA?

If there was a break in the dark clouds of the Depression in the early 1930s, it certainly occurred over French shipbuilding yards at Saint-Nazaire on 29 October 1932, the day the *Normandie* was launched. The very sight of this magnificent ship, and the drama of her launch, stirred the hearts of the great majority of the French populace. Built at a cost of some $60,000,000, not all agreed it was money well spent, and to her critics she became known as France's 'floating debt'. But from the moment the bottle of champagne smashed on her bows signalled the start of the launching process, *Normandie* was a ship destined to make headlines for the whole of her brilliant, but short, life afloat.

There is a moment during the launching of any ship when her fate hangs in the balance. For thirty seconds or so after she begins to move down the slipway, a ship is totally beyond the control of any human or mechanical intervention. As she races towards the water, nothing can stop her progress. If the launch team have done their job properly, the tons of drag chain welded to great brackets on the ship's hull will slow the rush downwards. If the amount of chain is not quite right, there's no telling what might happen! In the case of the *Normandie*, it appears that there was a miscalculation in the drag-chain equation – she raced down the heavily greased Saint-Nazaire slipway, entering the water at an estimated 17 knots. Hundreds of spectators were caught in the tidal backwash and were, literally, 'swept off their feet' into the River Loire in the excitement of the spectacular event. The *Normandie* was a sensation from that moment onwards.

This was a liner with seemingly endless distinctions: the first liner to exceed 1,000 feet in length, the first to surpass 60,000 tons, to be the fastest, to be the most luxurious and, typically for the French line, for its passengers to be the best fed and served. 'She is my favourite ship,' says John Maxtone-Graham. 'She is quintessentially, I think, *the* ocean liner. And why? Well, she was fast, she was smart, she was chic, she was beautifully designed. Her interiors were extraordinary, right up to the minute, the best that French art and artists could devise. She was just exquisite.'

Arnold Kludas agrees. 'The *Normandie* was my very favourite ship in external looks. She was so magnificent, so gigantic. She was fascinatingly beautiful. And, of course, she was so magnificent on the inside as well. She was a masterpiece of French architecture, French decoration and the French style of life.'

Prior to her launching there were endless rumours about what her name would be: *Jeanne d'Arc, La Belle France, General Pershing*, and even *Maurice Chevalier* were mentioned. However, *Normandie* was decided on, and what a beauty she was, with an extraordinary, raked profile dominated by a trio of red and black funnels. After the very last deckhouse and chain locker were placed aboard, her actual tonnage far exceeded the 60,000-ton mark. She was calculated to be an exceptional 79,000 tons, the largest liner of all time. But worrying for the French was the knowledge that Cunard was building not one but two 'superliners' that would be 'at least' 80,000 tons. If this was the case, the extravagant *Normandie* would soon be only the second biggest ship afloat, and that was not acceptable to the French. And so, during her first winter refit, in 1935–36, she was given a large, but unnecessary, deckhouse. This increased her tonnage to 83,400 tons. For the time being, *Normandie* was the largest ship afloat. The next question to be answered was whether she was also the fastest.

Normandie soon left little doubt about her speed, easily taking the Blue Riband from the *Rex* in the triumphant spring of 1935. She averaged 28.92 knots to New York, a triumph for the radical turbo-electric power unit, driving quadruple screws, that the designers had fitted. For almost a year *Normandie* ruled the North Atlantic.

Externally, this magnificent French liner had a very clean, almost 'swept' look. But it was her lavish interiors that received the greatest attention and accolades. The first-class restaurant, for example, was perhaps the most lavish at sea. It was a marvellous Art Deco creation of bronze, hammered glass and special Lalique fixtures. It sat 1,000 diners, rose three decks in height and offered menus that were beyond comparison. The Winter Garden featured live caged birds and lush greenery. The main lounge was covered by Dupas glass

OPPOSITE:
Normandie's first-class restaurant – 305ft long, 46ft wide and 3 decks high – was unquestionably the most extraordinary single public room ever placed on a ship.

panels and the chairs were upholstered in specially woven Aubusson tapestries. Similar to her grand forerunner, the *Ile de France*, all of the first-class suites and state-rooms on the *Normandie* were decorated in a different, distinctive style. Her top sun deck apartments consisted of a private terrace, four bedrooms, a living-room, quarters for a personal servant, trunk-rooms, a music salon and even a small private dining-room. The indoor pool consisted of 80ft (24m) of graduating mosaic-tiled levels.

It seemed that the only problem about the *Normandie* was that she was largely unprofitable. Overall, in her four years of sailing on the Atlantic, she averaged about 60 percent of her total capacity. Some have said that she was so overly luxurious that she actually discouraged more ordinary travellers. But like the *Bremen, Europa, Rex, Conte di Savoia* and the Cunard *Queen Mary*, which would soon make her debut on the North Atlantic, the *Normandie* was subsidized by her government. She was seen as a grand prestige piece and a great national symbol. She was a moving ambassador, an ocean-going museum, exhibiting floating magnificence. Her greatest moments came perhaps along New York City's West Side piers when she, together with the rival British, German and Italian liners, sat together in procession in a grand review. Passengers, visitors, officials and the dockers all had their views of the greatest, the finest, the very best. Unquestionably, the *Normandie* was almost always at the very top of the list when it came to public opinion of which was the greatest of them all.

The rusting hull of 'No. 534' had remained untouched for two years in John Brown's yards on the Clydebank until, after considerable lobbying with the British government, the Cunard management secured a loan of £3 million to complete '534', with 50 percent provided as working capital so that work could recommence immediately. A commitment was made to provide another £5 million if a sister ship was built.

The proviso to this arrangement was that Cunard had to merge with their traditional great rival, the White Star Line. It was an astute arrangement that the canny Board of Trade had worked out to prevent a second request on the public purse from financially troubled White Star. J. P. Morgan's interest in his International Mercantile Marine Co., (IMM), of which White Star had been part, had declined sharply after the First World War, with assets being disposed of to meet growing debts. The Royal Mail Group had acquired White Star in 1929, but it too had gone bankrupt. White Star needed a lot of financial help to survive. The government knew this, and the merger deal was a clever solution that provided both companies with an immediate answer to their financial problems. It also got large numbers of men back to work, stimulated British industry, and ensured that British prestige would be regained on the North Atlantic through the cohesive efforts of a financially secure company. This all came at a time when the people of Britain needed some sign of hope that the Depression years were drawing to a close. Their own liner, with the Blue Riband back in British hands, was to be a great morale booster for the entire nation.

When work started again on 'No. 534', in April 1934, clearing up the mess of two years' neglect was a mammoth task. Tons of rust had to be removed from the hull; gantries and cranes overhauled; cobwebs and giant birdnests dragged from every nook and cranny. It took months to get things back to normal again. But the spirit in the yard was immediately rekindled and, for the first time in almost two years, the men who were building this giant ship took home a pay packet. It was as though the whole of the Clydebank had breathed a sigh of relief. There was a sense of pride in the air again, and people smiled for the first time in almost twenty-four long, tough months.

The new Cunarder became, like the *Normandie* from across the Channel, a great national symbol of hope that the Depression would soon be over. While she was there in the shipyard, waiting to be finished, there was a guaranteed job for many people.

'There is a point above the town of Clydebank which is built on a hill,' recounts John Brown, 'and if you go up to the hill, you can look down, see the entire city and see the structure of the ship rising above it. Eventually, you would see the upper decks and then the funnels. It was quite a local feature. The Clydebank people were very, very proud of this,

being part of the great art of shipbuilding. No time was symbolically greater than during the building of the *Queen Mary*.' Of the workforce, John went on to remark, 'The men building the ship were as proud of their job as they could be. And certainly we who were in the design team, we knew we were on to something special.'

At last 'No. 534' was finished, ready for launching, and ready to take on a name. The launching date was set for September 1934. Cunard had kept the name secret, although betting around the Clydebank bars was that it would almost surely be *Victoria*. This seemed an obvious choice as it ended in 'ia', the company system of nomenclature. But, as the following story relates, even the best-laid plans often go astray for sometimes the most simple of reasons. It appears that the Cunard Chairman approached King George V, the grandson of Queen Victoria, and supposedly requested royal permission to name 'Britain's finest liner after her finest Queen'. His Majesty was said to have misunderstood and, with enthusiasm but not even thinking of his grandmother, announced that his wife would be delighted and he would tell her that evening. Under these circumstances the Chairman had little choice. The name *Queen Mary* became official. 'I attended the launch ceremonies and recall the royal platform,' added John Brown. 'King George V was suffering from chest problems and so, to protect him from the weather, we put up an actual glass screen on the launch platform. The royal party and official guests were behind it. But the day turned out to be so wet, lashing down, people getting soaked. So those screens were up all the time. I think it foiled photography for the occasion.'

Launching a ship of this size is an exacting business, with the major details worked out even before the keel is laid. There is no point in building a vessel and then finding out that it is almost impossible or dangerous to launch her, as Brunel had found out almost a century before with his huge *Great Eastern*, built on the banks of the Thames and, much more recently, with the dramatic charge down the slipways of the *Normandie*. John Brown had been given the task of ensuring a trouble-free launch for '534'. He recalls:

OPPOSITE:
The *Queen Mary* leaving Clydebank dock after her fitting out was completed in September 1934.

'I had done all the launching calculations. One of the first things you've got to do when you undertake a contract like that is to satisfy yourself that you can launch the ship. Then you have to decide whether two launchways will be sufficient to carry the weight of the ship. With some heavy naval ships they use four ways. We decided, no, we would have two ways. We had to dredge the river bottom to get sufficient depth. Eventually we did model tests with a mock-up of the river bottom in our tank to try and get the correct weight of drag chains. You have these huge bundles of drag chains, which are tipped over as the ship goes into the water and dragged to slow her down. And the question was, how much chain would we need. We did quite a lot of experimental work in our tank with a model of the ship, a mock-up of the bottom of the river, and various weights of drag chains in an attempt to gauge the resistance as the ship went down the launchways.

On the actual day of the launch it rained and the wind blew up the river, and the depth of water was far above what we'd expected. One of the key things when you're launching a ship is the depth of the water over the end of the launchways. If it's not sufficient, the ship could tip over, causing great damage. We did our calculations on the basis of having 8ft (2.4m) of water over the end of the launchways. On the day, we got about 11ft (3.3m), and it changed conditions completely. But we were prepared for that and the launchways were adjusted so that nothing went wrong. One of the big questions was how far the ship would travel once she was free of the launchways. We redid the calculations after the launch, using exactly the same basis as we had used with 8ft (2.4m) of water over the ways. We did the calculations again with the 11ft (3.3m) of water, and the distance that it travelled, by our calculations, was within 2ft (0.6m) of the actual distance run. This was hailed as one of the big achievements of the launching calculations.

The Queen herself launched the ship, using a bottle of Australian wine to send the mighty liner down the launchways. Bill Miller picks up the story: 'The twenty-eight words that Queen Mary spoke as she launched her namesake were the only words she ever said publicly as Queen.' Bill went on:

The Queen was a tremendous diarist and a great collector. She loved jade Buddhas, Fabergé eggs, and seventeenth-century Italian busts and footstools. And she'd go home and write pages in her diary about the acquisition of a little jade Buddha, or whatever. Well, the night when she got back to Balmoral after christening the world's largest and most luxurious liner, she sat down at her desk and wrote, 'launched the world's largest ship today. Too bad it rained'. And that's all she wrote about the event of the day. And a year and a half later, she and other members of the royal family went down to Southampton to see the fitted-out, finished *Queen Mary*. It was all very Art Deco and, well, light-years away from what the old Queen liked, but nonetheless she toured it with interest. She went back that night to Windsor Castle, and she wrote, 'Toured the new *Queen Mary* today. Not as bad as I expected.' Amazing!

It seemed that all of Britain, perhaps with the exception of their Queen, were fascinated by their new ship. Enthusiastically, they read about her 10,000,000 rivets, 2,000 portholes and 2,500sq ft (225sq m) of glass. She boasted 600 telephones, 700 clocks and 56 different kinds of wood in her interiors. While some areas of her decor leaned towards Art Deco, she was generally a very warm, inviting and appealing ship. Traditional and solid in the Cunard style, the new *Queen Mary*, however, appeared a little old-fashioned to many people, including Frank Braynard. 'The *Queen Mary*,' remarked Frank, 'was like an old-fashioned freighter . . . she didn't look anything like as glamorous and beautiful as the *Normandie* did, in my opinion. But inside was different,' he added, with a smile.

Her statistics were unprecedented in size and grandeur: 80,750 tons, 975ft (292.5m) long, with Parsons-geared turbines that developed almost 200,000hp driving 4 giant propellers, each weighing 35 tons. Her accommodation consisted of 776 in suites and cabin class, 784 in tourist class and 579 in third class. Two pieces of trivia that publicists felt compelled to add were:

The height of the *Queen Mary* from the keel to the top of the forward funnel is greater than the Niagara Falls. The sirens mounted on the forward funnel can be heard at a distance of at least ten miles, *and* the reverberations keep on going and can be detected from 50 to 100 miles away! However, keyed to lower bass 'A' they are so attuned that passengers on the ship will not be disturbed.

It would not be until May 1936, when *Queen Mary* made her maiden voyage, that the world would finally see if a British-built and owned ship could regain the prestige, and ultimately the Blue Riband, from their great rivals across the English Channel. Anglo/French rivalry had led to many a fierce battle in the past and the contest between *Normandie* and *Queen Mary* was shaping up as another memorable battle, in this case to be fought on the high seas of the stormy North Atlantic. The battle for domination of the North Atlantic would see records broken and history made.

NOTES
1 Robert Wall, *Ocean Liners*, Collins, 1978, page 212.
2 Maddocks, *op. cit.*, page 72.

The *Queen Mary* was a ship of statistics: 4 million rivets in her hull and upper decks, 600 clocks on board, 56 kinds of wood in the decoration and a rudder so large that two men could fit inside it.

CHAPTER THREE

THE
APPROACH OF ARMAGEDDON

The year 1930 was not much more than a decade after the end of the First World War. In spite of such well-meaning efforts as the League of Nations, nationalism was still very much in evidence, especially in Fascist Italy, in the soon-to-be Nazi Germany and also in the democracies of France and Britain. The United States was too busy putting its own house in order to play the game of transatlantic racing, but many European countries felt that a presence on the Atlantic run was necessary for national prestige, and that achieving pre-eminence in this might be worth paying for. By the mid-Thirties, the front-runners for size and speed were the British and the French, represented by the *Normandie* and the *Queen Mary*.

YOUTH AT THE PROW AND
PLEASURE AT THE HELM

The two great liners in many ways epitomized the national characteristics of France and Britain, at least as they were in the years between 1936 and 1939 when rivalry between the French Line and Cunard was at its height. Samuel Cunard would have approved of the way in which the Cunard directors kept firmly in mind the need for safety – and, of course, profit. Lavish display was all very well, as long as it attracted passengers.

The Cunard design philosophy had notably less *élan* than that of the French line. When planning their 'superships',

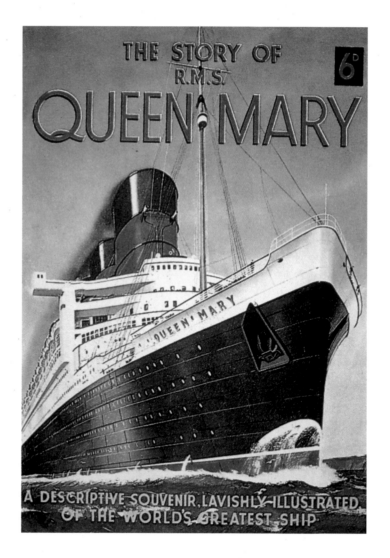

THE STORY OF
R.M.S.
QUEEN MARY
6D
A DESCRIPTIVE SOUVENIR, LAVISHLY-ILLUSTRATED, OF THE WORLD'S GREATEST SHIP

LEFT:
Expectedly, the new *Queen Mary* prompted newspaper and magazine articles, commemorative journals and, of course, books.

OPPOSITE:
Probably the greatest and most beloved of all Cunarders, the regal *Queen Mary*, flag-bedecked and glistening, slowly making her way up the Hudson River. The date is 1 June 1936.

The glittering Art Deco main dining hall on board the *Queen Mary* on her maiden voyage in 1936.

Cunard was far more conservative, their emphasis rooted in elements from their earliest days: efficiency, good service and overall passenger comfort. Cunard, however, did create the greatest transatlantic team ever: the first two-ship relay with weekly departures from London and New York. Their two liners, to be known ever afterwards as the 'Queens' were created especially for this passage and consequently they had to be not only very powerful but very large and strong as well.

The plans for *Queen Mary* were based on the splendid old *Aquitania* of 1914. The new ship, with three instead of four funnels, and a majestic rather than a modern look about her, was seen as far less pretentious or innovative than the glamorous *Normandie*. 'The *Normandie* had the most magnificent sweeping prow, like a clipper ship,' explained Frank Braynard. 'From then on, every liner built has had a similar bow. It had a tremendous impact on ship design. In addition to that, the *Normandie*'s bow had a lovely clean sweep up to the bridge. No air funnels, no anchor chains, no appurtenances.'

The $60 million (more than $600 million today)

Normandie was arguably the ultimate ocean liner of the thirties, and perhaps of the century. The culmination of a continuing series of lavishly designed and increasingly modern French Line passenger ships, the *France* of 1912, the *Paris* of 1921, the *Ile de France* of 1927, and the *Champlain* of 1932, her designer, Vladimir Yourkevitch took something from each of these in his search for perfection of shape, design, and performance.

The *Normandie* was a ship of the future. Her three huge red and black funnels diminished in height moving aft, the third being a dummy, functioning only as a ventilator. Her outdoor upper decks were meticulously cleared: not a ventilator, deckhouse or chain locker in sight. All these technical facilities were cleverly hidden from view. The exquisitely raked bow was a masterful conjunction of form and function, contributing significantly to the vessel's record speed. On the other hand, as Frank Braynard concludes, 'The *Queen Mary* was just exactly the opposite. In many ways, she was like an old-fashioned liner.'

'The *Queen Mary* was never intended to be a radical ship,' adds John Brown, and continues:

Cunard were very, very conservative in their outlook. They stuck to the tradition of ships they had built and were not very receptive to new ideas. At the time, for example, welding was coming in but Cunard would not hear of it. The *Queen Mary* had to have a riveted structure. And they wouldn't listen to any of the new welding techniques either. Even in the *Queen Elizabeth*, these techniques were only used to a very limited extent. The conservatism in exterior design originated with the owners. We had to follow Cunard practices. Internally, the French went for more modern decor. Cunard stuck again to more traditional ideas. In almost all ways, the *Normandie* represented the new age.

But in the all-important enterprise of attracting passengers, the French had not necessarily achieved quite the right ambience. As Frank Braynard says, 'The *Queen Mary* was very successful. *Normandie* was a failure. Nobody sailed on the *Normandie*, nobody knows why. People thought it was like living in a cathedral.' Certainly the *Queen Mary* was quite different, according to Bill Miller: 'The British ships had their sort of tufted chintz-like comfort about them. They had a smell of cleaning fluid and floor wax about them. And it worked. It wasn't an offensive smell, but it was a cosy, embracing smell.' The atmosphere was not quite as cosy for everyone. Kitty Carlisle, the American actress and singer, remembers her first voyage on the *Queen Mary*:

> I was so nervous, travelling alone. I was very young. And I always got terribly seasick on ocean liners. And they didn't have any Dramamine in those days . . . You just had to eat celery and they said to drink a little champagne, none of which did any good at all. So I remember the smell of the linoleum as I got to the ship made me feel sick before the ship left the dock.

In spite of, perhaps even because of, the owner's refusal to bow to fashion as viewed on the Continent, the new Cunarder became a great national symbol, a ray of hope in those meagre, unemployed times. She was especially symbolic, while she was being built, to the hard-hit regions near the Clyde.

Comfortable and a little old-fashioned, the *Queen Mary* had leather chairs and oversized sofas, lots of flowers, and the ritual of tea at 4pm every afternoon. Evidently the only widely known blemish was that she quickly became noted as a great 'roller' at sea, and transoceanic gossips reported that 'the *Queen Mary* could roll the milk out of a cup of tea'! There were rumours that she smashed enough of her crockery to make the potteries very happy supplying replacements.[1]

Ted Meech, a bell-boy in the *Queen Mary* when she sailed on her maiden voyage, remembers the British crowd at the dockside, desperate for souvenirs.

> They were tugging at you. 'Can I have a button?' They were trying to pull your buttons off . . . Of course you were very proud about it. I mean it was like being picked for your country . . . Yes, it was a great feeling . . . I mean today *Oriana* doesn't do for you what the *Queen Mary* did.

When the liner arrived in New York, the souvenir hunters had been busy again, collecting ashtrays, cutlery, pepper-pots, and even potted palms and paintings.[2] The *Queen Mary* steamed into New York Harbor for a rousing reception on her maiden voyage in May 1936. It was a year after the *Normandie* had arrived.

There was no Blue Riband on that maiden voyage. Safety and reliability had to be assured first. As the Cunard Chairman explained to a previously disappointed British public when, in August 1936, the *Queen Mary* did break the record:

> While we have let out the *Queen Mary* during this voyage we had an object in what we were doing. We are at the moment engaged in consideration of the *Queen Mary*'s sister ship. To help us to a proper consideration of the details of the machinery and the propellers the round voyage, such as the *Queen Mary* has run this fortnight, was of the greatest assistance.[3]

It was the first Atlantic crossing in under 4 days. She had done it in 3 days, 23 hours and 57 minutes but, behind the scenes, there were a few little problems to be solved. A few months later *Queen Mary* was withdrawn from service, and the engineers got to work. The hull was strengthened to reduce troublesome vibration, the huge propellers were replaced, and the funnels were rebuilt to cut down their emissions of soot.[4] Yet with all her faults, ordinary British people loved her. Bert Moody, born and brought up in the Queen Mary's home port of Southampton, says,

> It's funny, because the *Mary* was always much more popular than the *Elizabeth*. And I think the reason for this was that the *Mary* was the turning point in industry in this country in the early Thirties . . . and as a result she was really the star of redevelopment of a lot of industry in this country . . . If that's the reason, then it was an example to everybody at that time that . . . Britain's going to be all right.

The wealthy passengers loved her too.

There was an initial struggle with the French flagship for the Blue Riband and the kudos and popularity that went with it. *Normandie* regained the Blue Riband in 1937, with 3 days, 22 hours and 7 minutes, but the Cunard ship took the pennant in August 1938 and, for nearly fifteen years, it remained in British hands. *Queen Mary*'s record time was 3 days, 20 hours and 40 minutes.

In the late 1930s New York Harbor was the busiest port in the world, and the most glamorous. David Roach grew up in

FOLLOWING SPREAD, LEFT: *Normandie* arrives off Lower Manhattan for the first time, to the sounds of bellowing whistles and screeching sirens.

FOLLOWING SPREAD, RIGHT: A 1938 Nazi propaganda poster advertising KdF ('Strength Through Joy' movement) travel passes which offered cheap travel for German workers and their families.

89

New York, where his family was for many years in the tugboat business:

> We used to go out and sometimes my Dad would run the tug up alongside the tugs that were docking the ships at that time. And to get alongside one of those ships on an 80- or 90-ft (24- or 27-m) tug and look up at this massive piece of steel coming up with 1000 [people] waving to you from up on deck, it was something else. And I remember seeing the *Berengaria* that used to come in here right to Pier 92 on the north side. I saw the *Mauretania*. I remember seeing the great *Normandie* come in on one occasion. And of course I saw the old *Queens*, saw a lot of the American ships that were around in those days . . . Saw the Italian liners long before the *Michelangelo* and the *Raffaello* were built . . . Saw the German ships. Saw the great Grace liners . . . And I saw quite a few of them steaming up the harbor.

On special days, David's father would take him aboard some of the great ships.

> I can remember being on some of the ships early in the morning when they'd be breaking out the deck-chairs. In those days the deck-chairs were mahogany or hardwood. And there were the stewards out there wiping them down. There was no soot on them, no moisture: getting everything ready, put a blanket on it, so when the passenger came on, if he had a reserved one, they took him right to his reserved chair. It's gone. It's a piece of history in this harbor that those like myself . . . like my Dad and Grandad, it's a piece of history that's just gone.

The age of the 'superliner' might have continued further had it not been for the Second World War. Hamburg-Amerika Line had actually launched the first of three Atlantic 'wonder ships', the 41,000-ton, 1,322-passenger *Vaterland* in August 1940, and she and her 23.5-knot sisters would have greatly reinforced their owners' position on the Hamburg–New York run. But the 822ft (246.6m) *Vaterland* was laid up soon after launching and then destroyed during the Allied air raids on Hamburg Harbour in the summer of 1943.

Even more impressive was the North German Lloyd's plan to build an 80,000-tonner in the early 1940s. 'She was to be about the same size as the *Queen Mary, Queen Elizabeth* and *Normandie*, but with more powerful engines,' says Arnold Kludas. 'She would have had five screws. She would have won the Blue Riband for Germany and that was the primary intention. The Nazis would have paid happily for this triumph.' Initially to be called *Amerika*, this 1,070ft (321m) liner would have regularly crossed between Southampton (the day after leaving Bremerhaven) to New York in four days compared with the five days required by the *Normandie* and *Queen Mary*.

It was planned that this ship would carry 2,000 passengers: 400 in cabin class, 700 in tourist and 900 in third class. A model was prepared in 1938 and the keel-laying was scheduled for the autumn of 1939 in the presence of Adolf Hitler himself. But the outbreak of the war that September changed these plans and the project was temporarily shelved. Later, Hitler insisted that the project be revived, at least in the planning stages, and he suggested that the ship would be the first of a new fleet of 'superliners' for the intended merger of the Hamburg-Amerika Line and the North German Lloyd as the German-America Line. It was further planned that when the war was concluded victoriously, this first ship would be named the *Viktoria*.

It was in some ways odd that the Germans did not take much part in the competition for the Blue Riband in the late '30s, especially in view of Germany's traditional rivalry with Britain. Though *Bremen* and *Europa* had been contenders for the Blue Riband before *Normandie* appeared and set the fashion for modern liners with their two squat funnels and bulbous bows, they had been outclassed, at least in speed, since their launches in 1928 and *Bremen*'s double victory in 1933.

Germany may not have been equipped to compete with *Normandie* and *Queen Mary* at full throttle on the North Atlantic, but they were very interested in cruising in the later 1930s for their own very specific purposes. The 'Strength through Joy' idea started in 1934. In Germany itself, it was known as the 'KdF' (*Kraft-durch-Freude*). It was created and controlled by the propaganda division of the Third Reich, and Adolf Hitler took a personal interest in it. At least some of its

funds came from the confiscation of trades unions' finance, which had been sequestered after the Nazis came to power in 1933.

'Strength through Joy' ran an all-German cruise operation that offered inexpensive holiday voyages to national workers and, in particular, to members of the Nazi Party as well as their families. The idea was also, like the building of *Normandie* and *Queen Mary*, fuelled by the Depression. It was an alternative use for German ocean liners that otherwise might have been out of work and laid up in those lean times. Rather quickly, it became quite popular. Hans Prager, a German maritime historian, later wrote:

> For an enormously large number of 'national comrades', a sea journey in one of those big white ships was their first encounter with the sea and with sea travel altogether; for the great majority of them, it was also an event which few years earlier could not even have been thought about. Men and women, who during their lifetime had scarcely travelled beyond the provincial capital, were now seeing the Norwegian fjords, the Bay of Naples, the Canary Islands and the Icepack at Spitzbergen.[4]

It was generally thought for many years afterwards that the

on-board entertainment included political lectures and Nazi Party meetings, but according to Arnold Kludas this was not the case. Kludas adds, '70 per cent of the passengers on these cruises were workers and their families. No meetings were held on board. Perhaps the only intention was to have them spread the word afterwards of the good deeds of the Nazi movement.' However, Kludas also gives an account of a visit to London by one of the ships during the 1938 national elections to act as a polling station for Germans living in England. The visit interested British journalists; the propaganda value of the idea was evident even internationally.

The first cruise-ships were recruited from Germany's three major passenger fleets: the North German Lloyd, Hamburg-Amerika Line and Hamburg Sud-Amerika Line. Always decorated from stem to stern in signal flags, KdF pennants and Nazi banners, the fleet included such passenger ships as the *Dresden, Monte Olivia, Der Deutsche, Oceana* and the infamous *St Louis*, best remembered from her June 1939 voyage to Havana with Jewish refugees and later immortalized in both books and films, notably *The Voyage of the Damned.*

The Third Reich could not have been happier with the results of the 'Strength through Joy' scheme. The ships were filled to capacity. Within three years, by 1937, orders were placed for two specially designed, quite large passenger liners which, historically, rank as the first, big, all-cruise vessels ever built. The 25,000-ton *Wilhelm Gustloff*, launched at Hamburg, was commissioned in the spring of 1938. While actually owned by the so-called German Workers' Front, her cruise management and staffing were handled by the more experienced Hamburg Sud-Amerika Line. The slightly larger, although otherwise very similar, *Robert Ley* followed within a year, in the spring of 1939. She was managed by Hamburg-Amerika.

Both ships were run purely for passengers and carried no cargo whatsoever. Because of their leisure, all-cruise nature, they were comparatively slow ships, making just over 15 knots maximum. They were fitted with modern accommodation, extremely sophisticated fire safety systems and two very large searchlights, which were attached to the foremasts and mostly used to floodlight coastal areas for the enjoyment of the passengers. Perhaps the practice also appealed to German military intelligence, if any were by chance on board. Hans Prager added:

These ships were, in fact, remarkable in many respects. They became the pacesetters for construction of special cruiseships, even down to the present day. All 1,465 passengers were allowed to have outside cabins. And incidentally, the *Wilhelm Gustloff* was the first sea-going ship on which, according to Government instructions, the crew had to be accommodated in exactly the same manner as the passengers.[5]

Before the Second World War started, these two cruise-ships were used to bring home the soldiers of the German Legion and the Condor Legion from Spain at the end of the Spanish Civil War, in which General Franco had owed his eventual victory largely to German help. 'Otherwise,' says Professor Jürgen Rohwer, 'they had only peaceful uses during the uneasy Thirties.'

Perhaps modern passengers would have found the accommodation on the 'Strength through Joy' ships rather spartan. 'There was not much luxury in the cabins,' says Arnold Kludas, 'there was running hot and cold water, and there were four beds, and there was some space for the clothes. More comfort was not important, but the ship's general rooms were quite good accommodation.' Before long, Germany's workers had more to think about than their next cruise. Another world war was about to break out.

Since they came to office in 1933, the Nazis had pursued a policy designed, among other things, to establish Germany as the dominant world power by all means, including war. Domestically this had proved popular because enhanced production of armaments, in contravention of the Versailles peace treaty, had helped bring about full employment as well as restoring faith in German industrial skills. Although the British people may have felt initially reassured by Prime Minister Neville Chamberlain's 'piece of paper' which had promised peace in 1938, by the middle of 1939 neither the British nor the Germans had much doubt that they would

soon be at war with each other. Refugees hurried to escape from Europe to the comparative safety of Britain or the United States and the British dug air-raid trenches in London parks.

John Havers, then an official at Portsmouth, remembers the eerie weeks of August 1939, just before the war began:

> I'd actually gone out to visit the *Bremen*. She wasn't allowed in. I was actually seeing somebody off who was going to Germany. And then Germans were drunk with enthusiasm. Saluting, Hitler salutes all over the place. It was the most unpleasant ship visit I've ever made. I think they were all drunk with power or some equivalent to that. Buoyed up by Hitler's speeches. And they were all lining the decks with the salutes, saying we'll march against England and all that sort of thing. It was awful on the ship, absolutely appalling. I was so glad to get back on the tender.

TOTAL WAR

The first passenger-ship casualty of the Second World War was the British *Athenia*, a 13,850-tonner owned by the Glasgow-based Anchor Donaldson Line. Outward bound from Glasgow to Montreal, she was torpedoed and sunk on 3 September 1939, the very day on which Britain declared war on Germany, at a time when hostilities between Britain and Germany was only a few hours old. She carried 1,418 passengers, 300 of them Americans, and was unarmed and unescorted when the U-boat attacked. Some 112 passengers and crew perished. The loss of this ship, the first submarine victim of the Second World War, was against the emphatic order from the German High Command that no action should be taken against a liner for the time being. The German Naval Command reinforced the prohibition on the next day by

RIGHT:
The *Robert Ley* was the second of these 'Strength through Joy' liners. Commissioned in April 1939 she was sunk, with enormous loss of life, in March 1945.

OPPOSITE:
The *Queen Mary* being painted grey in New York prior to her 'secret' departure for Sydney and the commencement of her war duties. On the left, the *Normandie* lies idle, awaiting a decision on her future.

sending a signal to the effect that: 'The Führer has forbidden attacks on passenger liners sailing independently or in convoy.' The U-boat captain, Leutnant Lemp, claimed that he had believed the *Athenia* to be an armed merchant cruiser, but it was clear that Germany was likely to suffer international condemnation if the attack was admitted, so the tragic incident was denied by the Nazis during the entire duration of the war. This did not prevent the British from using the tragic incident as an example of German aggression, much as the sinking of the *Lusitania* had been used in the First World War.

Since American passengers had been lost on the *Athenia*, it was largely American sympathies that were enlisted to the British cause. Certainly, British naval manners were held to be exemplary (if outdated) when a British submarine commander surfaced to demand that the *Bremen* should stop its headlong dash back to the safety of Bremerhaven so that he could sink it. The *Bremen* did no such thing, and raced to port as befitted a sometime Blue Riband holder, easily outrunning the submarine.

With war declared, passenger services on the North Atlantic ground to a halt. All that remained were the still-neutral American liners, the two largest being the sister ships *Washington* and *Manhattan*, which turned immediately to evacuation service, first from France, later from Italy, and finally from Portugal. The Italians continued their commercial services as well, supposedly a symbol of Mussolini's neutrality. Except for neutrality markings painted along their sides, the 'superliners' *Rex* and *Conte di Savoia* continued in 'normal' Atlantic service until Mussolini revealed himself as Hitler's ally.

In the autumn of 1939, New York – among other ports – was a quiet haven to a mighty fleet of suddenly idle liners. The *Normandie* and the *Ile de France* lay in adjacent berths to the already grey-painted *Queen Mary*. On the opposite shores of the Hudson, at Hoboken, the Dutch flagship *Nieuw Amsterdam* was caught in a similar limbo. She was diverted into temporary Caribbean cruise service, away from the lurking dangers of the North Atlantic. Soon the brand-new, second *Mauretania*, launched in 1938, arrived at New York's

'Luxury Liner Row', having been considered far too great a risk alongside the Liverpool docks, and the *Ile de France*, under the care of ten Moran tugs, was moved away to an even more remote berth, on distant Staten Island.

Meanwhile, on the other side of the Atlantic, at Southampton, John Havers, in uniform by late September 1939, recalls his first visit to the docks in wartime:

> I saw the liners *Athlone Castle, Alcantara* and *Pennland*, but now as troopers. Later, I attended the group sailing of the *Athlone Castle, Alcantara, Empress of Australia* and *Franconia*. In October, there were ninety-eight ships in Southampton, among them the *Aquitania, Capetown Castle, Orcades, President Harding, Somersetshire*, seventeen cross-Channel steamers and lots of requisitioned yachts.

The great liners were soon transformed into hardworking troop transports. The 1,220-passenger *Nieuw Amsterdam*, for example, carried a total of over 370,000 troops during the war or an average of 8,599 men, about seven times more than her peacetime load, per voyage. The initial task of removing her beautiful public rooms and cabins was done largely by Chinese labour at Singapore, but much of the fittings suffered grievous damage through haste, carelessness and misuse. Furniture, decorations and carpets remained in piles along the Singapore docks for weeks and in all weathers. Later, the furnishings were shipped to Australia and then to San Francisco before going home to Rotterdam in 1946. The ship's transformation included the stripping of all 'C' deck cabins, which were replaced by more than 1,000 canvas hammocks. The Grand Hall became a duplex dormitory for 600 in three-tier bunks, the converted theatre slept 386 and each former first-class suite contained sleeping accommodation for 22 men.

In the East, there were more radical measures in preparation for war. Japan's largest liners yet, the 27,700-ton sister ships *Kashiwara Maru* (built by Mitsubishi) and *Izumo Maru* (built by Kawasaki) were intended to carry passengers for the Olympic Games planned for Tokyo in 1940 on the Yokohama–San Francisco run, but were never even launched as such. Instead, in August 1940, well over a year before the war in the Pacific had broken out, the Japanese Navy took over the building contracts and had the two 722-ft (216.6-m) long hulls completed as aircraft carriers. As the Japanese Admiralty had been involved in their design, the conversion proceeded smoothly and both were launched in June 1941; they were renamed *Junyo* and *Hiyo* respectively. After taking part in many operations, *Junyo* exploded and sank in 1944, and *Hiyo*, much damaged by bombing, was sent for scrap in 1946.

One of the most daring ocean escapes during the Second World War was that of the world's largest liner, Cunard's *Queen Elizabeth*. She was due to have her commercial maiden crossing in April 1940, an appointment she was clearly fated not to keep. As Britain's war machine was started, her final construction and outfitting were halted. There were even suggestions that she should be sold off to the Americans, who, it was said, would probably convert the 1,031-ft (309-m) ship to an aircraft carrier. Up on the Clyde, where she was being fitted out, warships now took precedence. But the mighty *Queen Elizabeth* remained at her builder's dock in that first tense winter of war and amid increasing danger. Worrying reports from intelligence agents revealed that the Nazis planned to bomb or at least sabotage her, and that German agents were already in the Glasgow area. In response, Winston Churchill, then First Lord of the Admiralty, ordered her away from British shores, partly to make room to refit the battleship *Duke of York*.

The huge bulk of the *Queen Elizabeth* could only leave her fitting out basin and navigate safely down the Clyde on an especially high tide, at the earliest date of 26 February 1940. On the next high tide that day the great battleship *Duke of York* would slip into the basin just vacated by the liner.[7] A deliberate rumour was spread that the new *Queen Elizabeth* would travel down to Southampton for drydocking. In doing so, she would have to pass through the English Channel, and the Nazis, upon hearing this, planned to have the Luftwaffe bombers waiting. They were encouraged when their agents reported that packing cases full of supplies for the final fit-out were arriving at the George V dry dock in Southampton, and that hotel rooms nearby were being reserved for the John

Brown technicians. The harbour officials at Southampton were equally misled.[8]

On a dark February day, the largest liner in the world, painted a sombre grey that matched the weather, was nudged out into the Clyde. By the time she was safely anchored it was dark. She was due to sail out through the anti-submarine boom at eight o'clock on the morning of 2 March. At seven o'clock the King's Messenger arrived with her sealed sailing orders, not to be opened until she was at sea. The crew were told she would not be sailing for Southampton, though not what her destination was; some preferred not to set out on an ocean trip, but those who stayed would get inconvenience money. Also on board were many engineers who would supervise the as yet untried vessel's many systems, for this would be a sea trial as well as a maiden voyage.

The betting on board favoured Halifax, Nova Scotia, as her destination, but after she had travelled for 200 miles (300km) with her escort of destroyers, *Queen Elizabeth* steamed off alone as fast as she could go for her real destination: the port of New York. Meanwhile, frustrated German bombers buzzed angrily over the Solent, where she should have been sailing en route for Southampton.

The Nazis were furious – they had lost their chance. Westbound, blacked out, in the tightest security, the liner

The *Queen Elizabeth* leaving Clydebank in February 1940 to begin the most unusual maiden voyage in liner history.

RIGHT:
Once the exteriors had been transformed, the interiors of the luxury liner *Queen Mary* were also made ready for war. Areas where once the rich and famous relaxed were turned into a hospital ward in preparation for the transportation of troops from Sydney to the Middle East in 1940.

RIGHT:
The *Queen Mary* moves down Sydney Harbour with an escort of small craft on her way to the Middle East in 1940. The *Aquitania* can be seen behind her, also ready to sail.

travelled without revealing her destination. Speed and secrecy were her only defence. On board, a ghostly crew of about 400 instead of the full complement of 1,296, with state-rooms to themselves, were well aware that they depended on the speed and agility of a ship that had never been to sea before. Their faith was justified. On the morning of 7 March she was spotted by the crew of a TWA airliner. There was no disguising the huge ship as she approached New York. Grey and already rusting as she was, the *New York Post* gave her an enthusiastic welcome:

> As she slowly made her way up river, she was accorded the tumultuous welcome befitting the most distinguished representative of maritime royalty ever to reach America's shores. Thousands of spectators thronged the windows and tops of West Side buildings. More than a dozen planes circled overhead and dipped time and time again in salute, while scores of tugboats churned the water on all sides of the great grey majesty with whistles and sirens wide open.

Even allowing for a little exaggeration, it seems New York was pleased to see the giant new Cunard 'superliner'. She went directly to Cunard's terminal at the foot of West 50th Street and there joined the already idle *Queen Mary* and *Normandie*. For about two weeks, the three largest ocean liners ever built were together.

Queen Mary moved out of New York on 21 March, without most of her luxurious furnishings and painted naval grey. Next month she arrived in Cape Town after zigzagging across the South Atlantic, and on 17 April arrived at her destination, Sydney. Sydney and Singapore were the only ports in the eastern hemisphere capable of handling her. Moored to a buoy in the middle of Sydney harbour, the great liner was soon surrounded by a busy fleet of small craft. By 5 May, in a working time of only fourteen days, the Australian workers from Cockatoo Docks had fitted her out with wooden bunks, hammocks and scores of extra latrines, in preparation for the first 5,000 soldiers to sail on her as a troopship.[9] The Australians were on their way to the battlefields of southern Europe and North Africa. Hitler had by now established an iron grip on most of the rest of Europe.

In New York, *Queen Elizabeth* was quickly fitted out with the basic equipment still missing on board – electric cabling, light fittings, and so on. There were even more basic needs: her launch gear was still fixed to her hull, due to the unceremonious haste of her exit from British waters, and her bottom was foul after two continuous years in the water. But no dry dock large enough was available to her – except in Singapore. The liner was built for five-day voyages, so for such a long journey she would have to refuel twice en route. Accordingly, two stops were arranged, at the British ports of Trinidad and Cape Town, and *Queen Elizabeth* arrived safely in Singapore after a three-week trip. The local population were complacent and unconvinced of the urgency of the situation, and in turn some of the liner's crew (not regular members, it was claimed) ran riot in the city's nightspots. It was not a happy stay. The *Queen Elizabeth* arrived for her refit as a troop-ship in Sydney in February of 1941, and would now work on the passage from Suez to Sydney with the *Queen Mary*.

Both the ships had been equipped to keep passengers warm on the North Atlantic run, and now they were regularly crossing the Equator carrying many thousands of men in conditions of heat that verged on the intolerable. The troops were packed in twice as densely as her peacetime design had intended. Neither ship had air conditioning nor even adequate ventilation, and the Australians, on their way north to battle, were disinclined to put up with it. Fights and near-mutinies broke out on those voyages; but on the return voyage to Australia things were even worse. The liners were carrying enemy prisoners of war, many of them wounded, who succumbed to the heat. Passing through the inferno of the Red Sea there could be sea burials every four hours.[10]

'When we were carrying full divisions of troops, we rotated bunks on the *Queens*,' recalls Captain Michael Dodds, who served with Cunard at the time. 'One bunk had eight-hour rotations so you used the bunk three times in twenty-four hours. One guy got out at eight o'clock in the morning, a chap got in, and so on and so forth. When we sailed with Australian troops during the early part of the war, we used palliasses in large dormitories. A palliasse is a mattress filled

100

with straw. In the hot weather of the Indian Ocean, ventilation in the lower-deck areas was quite terrible. There was never enough air.' Not only air was in short supply. 'The water supply was very poor . . . so they were rationed. And the water came on, I think it was seven to seven-thirty in the morning throughout the ship, everybody, crew, troops, didn't matter who it was. And I think it was six-thirty to seven at night. And they got through tremendous quantities of water in that time.'

For the *Queen*s, 1941 was the year of the Sydney to Suez shuttle. But on 7 December 1941, the day on which Japan bombed Pearl Harbor, priorities were revised. The *Queen*s returned to their North Atlantic run, but first ferried 20,000 American troops to an Australia severely weakened by the temporary absence of her own men in the northern hemisphere.

The Americans now enthusiastically took on the task of trebling the huge liners' capacity for carrying troops from 5,000 to 15,000. The British handed over both ships to them to use as they saw fit, with Britain paying the bills but getting, in return, the benefit of the American troops.[11] Each *Queen* could carry the equivalent of a division, and usually did, with the record at 16,683 troops on the *Queen Mary* in July 1943. The log entry was terse, in maritime style: 'New York to

Winston Churchill was undoubtedly the most frequent *Queen Mary* passenger during the war. He crossed the North Atlantic under great secrecy and with great security for personal meetings with Franklin D. Roosevelt.

America every time she docked there . . . We were all briefed when we first got on board that if you fall overboard we'll throw you a lifebelt, and that's it. She's not going to stop under any circumstances. There were too many lives at risk.

By the end of the war the two Cunard ships had carried far more troops than they would ever carry civilian passengers. Winston Churchill, more than once a passenger himself across the wartime Atlantic, concluded: 'Built for the arts of peace and to link the Old World with the New, the *Queen*s challenged the fury of Hitlerism in the Battle of the Atlantic. Without their aid the day of final victory must unquestionably have been postponed.'[13]

Though they were certainly the most famous, many other liners did as faithful and arduous a job as the *Queen*s. And some passenger ships took on unique tasks during the war years. After the fall of Holland in May 1940, the seat of the Dutch government in exile was moved to a troop-ship, Holland America's *Westernland*. For two months, while anchored off Falmouth in England, she was the headquarters to 800 officials under the direction of Prince Bernhard, the husband of Crown Princess Juliana. Cunard's *Franconia* served as Churchill's command centre during the Yalta conference. P&O's *Ranpura* became a floating workshop and repair centre for the British Admiralty, while the American liner *Ancon* became a communications ship in time for the Japanese surrender in August 1945.

During the European war most of the use of liners as troop-ships was on the Allied side, since the Axis powers had less need of them. Germany requisitioned the *Bremen* and the *Europa* to provide accommodation; but, as Arnold Kludas explained, Germany required troop-ships only for her invasion of Norway. In the Mediterranean her new Italian allies provided transport, and continental Europe as a whole could be comfortably reached by road or rail.

Arnold Kludas:

The *Bremen* and *Europa* were accommodation ships at Bremerhaven in the beginning of the war. But then the Nazis decided to invade Britain in Operation Sea Lion. Some officers in the German Army believed that the *Bremen* and *Europa* should

Gourock (Clyde), 16,683 souls on board. New York 25 July 1943, Gourock 30 July 1943, 3,353 miles, 4 days, 20 hours 42 minutes. 28.73 knots. The greatest number of human beings ever embarked on one vessel.'[12] There were lifeboats and rafts for only 8,000 – but this was total war.

After training as an RAF navigator in Canada, Dennis Andrews returned to England on the *Queen Mary*. He took his turn as lookout on the wing of the great liner's bridge:

She was very heavily armed with anti-aircraft guns, all over. And, in addition, there was one big gun at the back, I think it was a four-inch gun, presumably in case she was attacked by a surface raider of some sort. But her main defence was her speed. The dining-rooms were busy all day from morning to night feeding everybody in rotation. And as fast as one lot went out the next lot were waiting and came in. But we got two very good meals a day indeed, because of course all the food came from become big-capacity transports carrying thousands of troops each and heavy equipment like tanks as well. In preparation, some rebuilding work was done. Their promenade decks were opened in the front to allow tanks and artillery to enter. But some Naval officers and engineers from the North German Lloyd realized that with tanks on the upper decks, the ships might easily capsize. Some trials were made and this was confirmed. But they were to be used as troop transports. We have documents from that period – rules for the soldiers, emergency steps and procedures if the ships were attacked. But then they could never have landed on British beaches as some suggest. Sensibly, they could only be taken into service when British harbours were in German hands and they could land at a pier.

The 32,500-ton North German Lloyd liner *Columbus* did not survive to become a troop-ship. Her crew scuttled her 400 miles off the US coast in 1939 rather than let her fall into British hands.

COUNTING THE COST

The competition for national prestige had produced the largest, fastest, most powerful passenger-carriers the world had ever seen. These monstrous pieces of machinery enabled whole armies to move distances in days or weeks, which had taken Alexander the Great, Julius Caesar and Wellington months or years. But progress has a price that must be paid. In the years between 1940 and 1945, a third of the world's liner fleet was destroyed. Modern company terminals, such as those for the Holland America Line at Rotterdam and for the French at Le Havre, were turned into twisted masses of rubble.

Even uncompleted vessels could not escape their fate. The largest Swedish liner yet built, the 29,300-ton *Stockholm*, was still under construction at Monfalcone, Italy, when the Second World War started. She was launched on 10 March 1940, appearing quite normal in her commercial colouring. But shortly afterwards, Mussolini's government seized the 1,350-passenger ship and then ordered her to be finished as the high-capacity troop-ship *Sabaudia*. Her brief life ended during an Allied air attack on Trieste in July 1944. Briefer yet,

Norway's 18,600-ton *Oslofjord* was only two years old when she fell victim to a magnetic mine in December 1940.

The most horrific loss in the early part of the war was of a Cunarder, the 16,200-ton *Lancastria*. While evacuating troops from France in June 1940, she was attacked by Nazi dive-bombers and sank within twenty minutes after a bomb exploded inside the vessel. Over half of the 6,000 troops on board perished. On 2 November 1942, while on an Allied voyage from South Africa to New York, the 10,900-ton Dutch motorliner *Zaandam* was struck by two Nazi torpedoes 400 miles off the Brazilian coast. She sank within ten minutes. An American naval vessel rescued only three survivors eighty-two days later. Their endurance against the open seas was then the greatest on record. A near-tragedy involved another Holland America liner, the *Volendam*, assigned, in the summer of 1940, to the child evacuation scheme from Britain to the United States and Canada. On 30 August, with 335 children and 271 adult passengers on board, she was torpedoed 300 miles off the Irish coast. Sinking by the bow, the passengers and crew left the liner, miraculously with the loss of only one life. The *Volendam*'s bow was awash, and the 579-ft (174-m) ship only barely afloat. She was taken in tow and brought to the Isle of Bute where temporary repairs were made before she was taken to Birkenhead shipyard for more thorough patching up. At that shipyard a second torpedo was found embedded in the hull. Had it exploded on impact, there would have been many fewer survivors.

The tragic blemish to the *Queen Mary*'s otherwise impeccable record was her collision, on 2 October 1942, with the escort cruiser HMS *Curacoa*. Off the coast of northwest Ireland, the *Curacoa* and four British Royal Navy destroyers were to escort the giant liner for the remaining day's journey to the Clyde. Both the Cunarder and the *Curacoa* were sailing at top speeds. While the cruiser was sailing at about 27 knots, the liner was sailing at 30 or 31 knots, and may have gradually gained on the *Curacoa*. The *Queen Mary* continually changed course according to a secret schedule, making an almost impossible target for a U-boat. The cruiser eventually, to the consternation of the liner's officers, disappeared from view beneath the *Mary*'s foredecks.

However, Captain Boutwood, on the bridge of the *Curacoa* had escorted the liner three times before, and Captain Illingworth, on the *Queen Mary*, was sure the cruiser's captain knew what he was doing. But there was a heavy swell, both ships were travelling at high speed, and a minor miscalculation suddenly became a fatal error.

Allin Martin was a young wireless telegrapher on the cruiser on that fateful day. Summoned by a colleague who thought he might like a photograph, Martin came out on deck:

> All I could see advancing was a sort of big wall of water like Niagara [Falls], I should say about 150yd (135m) away. Almost blotted out the sky. Realizing it was no time for photography – I don't know what happened to the camera – I dived inside. At that point in time the impact came. She threw us over on to our starboard side on to our beam ends, so that we were actually standing on the starboard bulkhead instead of the deck . . . As I emerged on to the deck the signalman came hurtling down from the bridge. 'Come on,' he said, 'Let's get out of this.' I said, 'Has abandon ship gone?' And his response, as far as I can remember, was, 'Abandon ship be buggered. The skipper's gone already.' And he had. So we scrambled down . . . and I remember at the time looking astern and there was just nothing there. The stern had gone already, disappeared, sunk . . . And by this time I could spot that our tanks had been ruptured and we were swimming in – or we would soon be swimming in – pure fuel oil. So I made for the perimeter. Swimming on my way out, one minute you were 25ft (7.5m) up in the air, and the next down in the trough . . . I remember at one point a boot, as if someone had carefully placed it on the water, and it sailed quite serenely by. And then there was something about as big as a coconut and at the time I thought it was a decapitated head. And in my panic . . . to get away from this I took quite a lot of water in. Turned on my back just in time to see the *Curacoa*, or what was left of her, about 50ft (15m) of bow, pointing vertically into the air. There was still a figure clambering over the wreckage. Just as she went under the whole bow exploded and threw a shower of debris into the air. We said afterwards this was probably the air inside being forced up as she went under. By this time there was just debris, bodies,

swimmers, everything, floating in the water. One of our stokers actually said that for three hours he was kept afloat by a case of New Zealand butter.

After three hours, during which the few survivors clung to a flotation device and (to Martin's astonishment) sang a number of hymns, they were picked up by one of the escort destroyers which had turned back to rescue them. Once on the destroyer, Martin was exhausted, but recovered before long:

> I felt reasonably well and in fact I went along to the WT [wireless telegraphy] office where they gave me a couple of stiff tots and I began to feel quite euphoric, you know. After about half an hour or so I decided to go for a walk on the upper deck. And the feeling of euphoria quickly evaporated because I could see all these lines of bodies that were being conveyed back for burial.

The *Queen Mary*'s bows had sliced through the cruiser's 3in (7.5cm) armour-plating and cut the ship in half. Only 101 sailors survived; 338 perished. As always during the war, the *Queen Mary* was under emphatic orders never to stop, not even in an instance such as this. A U-boat might easily be lurking and a slowed, or worse still, stopped troop-ship presented the perfect target. After the collision, the *Mary*'s speed was reduced to 15 knots and emergency repairs to her dented bow, using several tons of concrete, were made at Gourock by special crews sent over from the John Brown yard at Clydebank. With no dry-dock space available in Britain, full repairs to the *Queen Mary* had to be made in the United States. She was re-routed to Boston on her next crossing, then on to New York, where she lay idle at Pier 90 for a month and resumed sailings on 8 December, leaving New York Harbor with 10,389 GIs aboard.

In 1945, Allin Martin had to take a ship home from New York:

> I came back on the *Queen Mary*. And at the time there were several officers still on board who had been there when the tragedy happened and they said all they could feel at the time was the slightest bump, no great impact whatsoever. They would hardly have known anything had happened.

Captain Michael Dodds, then serving with Cunard, notes:

> There was a major inquiry after the *Queen Mary–Curacoa* collision. The relatives of those lost sued both the Admiralty and Cunard for compensation. The case finally went to the House of Lords in London and finally was decided against the Admiralty 75 percent and Cunard 25 percent. It was the biggest case against the Admiralty ever known. But it remained a major incident during the war. The Officer of the Watch on the *Queen Mary* at the time of collision was hounded by the media for many years after the war ended.

The war years were extremely destructive to the world's passenger liners, especially to the 'superliner' class. The *Empress of Britain*, attacked by enemy bombers and then torpedoed, sank in the eastern Atlantic in the autumn of 1940. She was the largest Allied merchant ship of the entire conflict to be lost.

Great liner names from the Axis powers were erased from the record-books as well. The *Bremen* was set afire by an unhappy crew member while she was lying at her Bremerhaven berth in March 1941. Her twisted remains were later cut up and sent to Nazi munitions plants. The big Italian liners were in the Mediterranean, and targets for the Allies. The *Conte di Savoia* was sunk by American bombers in Venice on 11 September 1943.[14] The *Rex* was sunk by British rocket-firing Beaufighters (two-engined night fighters) to prevent the Germans sinking her to blockade the harbour at Trieste in September 1944.[15] Dennis Andrews was a young navigator on one of the Beaufighters:

> She was 51,000 tons, of course, and an infinitely bigger target than we were accustomed to. Much easier to hit, for that matter. We were on stand-by until about four o'clock in the afternoon when we were suddenly told 'action stations', and about five o'clock we were airborne. And then we came out on the coastline and there we saw the town of Capodistria and Trieste, the big city beyond, and in between, in an inlet, was the *Rex*, our target, this big ship still in her original paintwork. And then, once we had lined up on her, the Mustangs went in first to strafe any ack-ack positions. We didn't see any, actually. And then we came in firing rockets, of course, and by this time the Trieste harbour

guns were firing ack-ack at us, and there were big bursts of black smoke from the ack-ack shells. And we dived down. That is the most vulnerable position, of course, in a rocket attack because you have to point the aircraft straight at the target. And then between our eight aircraft, sixty-four rockets were fired into her. We used rockets which were slim, like pencils, for anti-shipping work. And the beauty of them was that they were reputed to come out of the far side faster than they went in because the rocket motor was accelerating the whole time. Certainly they made a hell of a hole, and that was what let in the water.

Andrews remembers how he felt about the need to destroy the liner:

> She still looked big and beautiful actually, and it seemed sad that one had to sink something of that sort. But at the same time this was war, the war had been going on for five years. And during the war you can't really question the target and say that ship is too beautiful to sink . . . and so if we were told to sink it, then we would do our best to sink it.

But perhaps the most devastating loss among the world's 'superliners' was the tragic fire and sinking of the magnificent *Normandie*. When the war started in September 1939, she was laid up on the north side of New York's Pier 88, at the foot of West 48th Street. She might have become a high-capacity military troop-ship, like those other giants, the *Queen Mary* and *Queen Elizabeth*, or even a completely rebuilt aircraft carrier as suggested by several American newspapers and magazines. She was officially seized by the US government in December 1941, just after the Japanese attack on Pearl Harbor. The Americans planned to convert the giant French liner to a troop-ship capable of carrying 15,000 troops. She would be renamed the USS *Lafayette*. Work was in progress when, on 9 February 1942, a fire erupted. Sparks from a workman's acetylene torch ignited a pile of kapok lifejackets and triggered the blaze. The ship was evacuated as the fire spread. Huge clouds of orange-brown smoke covered midtown Manhattan as the 83,400-ton *Normandie* burned.

Frank Braynard was there:

> When I came out of the subway the entire sky was brown with

While the fire which destroyed the *Normandie* was devastating, too much fire-fighters' water was poured on to the great ship and she capsized within twelve hours through the sheer weight of water.

the smoke from the *Normandie*. I found Vladimir Yourkevitch in the crowd. He was the designer of the hull of the ship. And he had just been to see Admiral Adolphus Andrews, who was the Navy man in charge, and he said, 'I told him, let me on board. I can find the seacocks blindfolded. I will open the seacocks. The ship will sink three feet and be perfectly level.' And Andrews said, 'This is a Navy job.' And that was the end of the *Normandie*.

Maddening excitement led to miscalculation. Overzealous fireboats continuously and haphazardly poured tons of water on to the burning 1,028-ft (308.4-m) vessel. The weight was too much. In the early hours of the next day, she capsized – lying on her side, like a beached whale, in New York City's backyard, just as Yourkevitch had feared. Frank Braynard says: 'Oh, I was sick, absolutely sick. She was so far ahead of the *Queen Mary* in style, in beauty, in elegance, in interior, in everything. To see her destroyed there through the stupidity of a naval admiral just killed me.' Even the staid *New York Times* wrote, 'The sight of her hurts the human eye and heart.'[16]

Lying on her side, she presented a very difficult salvage task. All of her upper parts – the masts, the three huge funnels and the upper decks – had to be removed as pumps emptied water out of the vast hull. In all, it took fifteen months to do the job and cost a staggering $19 million.[17] She was finally declared surplus by the US government just after the war ended in 1945. A year later, she was sold for scrap to a local firm in New York Harbor, at Port Newark, New Jersey. In the end, her remains fetched a pathetic $161,680.

The 'Strength through Joy' cruise-ships *Wilhelm Gustloff* and *Robert Ley* were also casualties. Both ships were used as hospital-ships in the early part of the war and then as floating barracks in occupied Poland. In the end they were destroyed within two months of one another in the final phase of conflict, in the winter and spring of 1945. The *Wilhelm Gustloff* was torpedoed on 30 January by a Soviet submarine and then capsized while evacuating the so-called Eastern Territories of Poland and East Prussia in the face of rapid Soviet advances. It was part of the greatest evacuation by sea in history. According to Professor Jürgen Rohwer, two million people were evacuated to the West, and only some 20,000 were lost, about a quarter of them on the *Wilhelm Gustloff*. Three torpedoes struck her, and she sank in twenty minutes. Her loss ranks as the worst tragedy in maritime history; at least 5,200 refugees, prisoners, wounded soldiers and crew perished in the icy waters. This terrible disaster has since been the subject of several German books and films, but – quite surprisingly – has been given comparatively scant attention abroad. Her sister ship, the *Robert Ley*, was bombed during an Allied air raid on Hamburg in March 1945.

Another staggering German casualty was the former flagship of the Hamburg Sud-Amerika Line, the 27,600-ton *Cap Arcona*. She had been left in home waters after the war began in September 1939, but suffered one of the most hideous fates of any ship. At first used as an accommodation ship for the German Navy at occupied Gdynia (now again a Polish port), she went back to sea in January 1945 as part of the evacuation of the so-called German Eastern Territories. She carried 26,000 refugees in three voyages. That April, *Cap Arcona*, while anchored in Lubecker Bay, was gradually

loaded with over 5,000 prisoners from concentration camps and almost another 1,000 including guards, camp followers of the SS, and wounded soldiers, in addition to crew members. According to Arnold Kludas, the old liner and a small freighter anchored nearby were unable to move because of lack of fuel, but survivors have recently stated that *Cap Arcona* was towed into midstream by tugs.[18] On 3 May, both ships were attacked by British planes firing rockets and set on fire. *Cap Arcona* capsized with the loss of well over 5,000 lives. A couple of days later Germany surrendered. Some commentators feel that the British must have known of *Cap Arcona*'s sad cargo, but Himmler had only days before issued an order that concentration camp prisoners were not to fall into enemy hands alive. The captain of the *Cap Arcona* had also been threatened with instant execution because of his initial refusal to embark the prisoners, which suggests that their removal and execution was a matter of urgency. In fact, hundreds of prisoners had been shot by German military personnel on nearby beaches, and it seems likely that the

The largest, fastest and certainly the most luxurious of the German liners on the South American run: the superb, three-funnel *Cap Arcona* is seen berthed at Hamburg. She was destroyed and sunk in a British air attack only days before the German surrender. Over 5,000 concentration camp prisoners on board died.

same fate awaited those on the old liner. The British evidently regarded the mission, in which other shipping was attacked and destroyed, as a routine operation to prevent the escape of troops to northern ports. As Arnold Kludas says, 'It is absolutely not understandable. It is one other tragedy of total war.'

Between January and May 1945 the Germans lost twelve of their largest liners; as well as the *Wilhelm Gustloff, Robert Ley* and *Cap Arcona*, there were also the *Berlin, Steuben, Monte Rosa, Hansa, Hamburg, Monte Olivia, New York, General Osorio* and *Deutschland*. On the other side of the world, the Japanese passenger fleet was in ruins as well. Only one passenger ship, the 11,000-ton *Hikawa Maru*, survived and was eventually returned to her owners, the NYK Line, by her American captors.

When the war ended in Europe in May 1945, it seemed half the world wanted to go home. The war against Japan was still blazing in the Pacific, but there were thousands of

The *Queen Elizabeth* is shown arriving home with returning troops. Groups of uniformed women – Wacs, Wrens and the like – wave greetings to the soldiers along the crowded outer decks.

Australians who were bound for home, some after years in prisoner-of-war camps. So, battered and rusty, the great liners had a last few duties to perform. Captain Michael Dodds tells of a voyage with Australian, New Zealand and American troops going home on the *Mauretania*. Dodds went off one evening to visit relatives in Pearl Harbor. He says that when he returned to the ship:

> This officer I was relieving said to me, 'Thank God you're back. We're in a hell of a mess. There are troops on board, we don't know whether they're American, New Zealand, or what. They've all changed uniforms. Nearly all drunk. They've all got bottles and they're all over the ship' . . . Six o'clock, Captain Woollatt says, 'Let her go aft,' . . . And we sailed, bound for Wellington. Well, we had then to try and sort out carefully how many we had, how many were left behind, how many Americans we had aboard and so on.

Eventually the *Mauretania* reached the end of the voyage in Sydney, just in time for VJ (Victory in Japan) day. Dodds continues:

> The pubs opened and stayed open, and they drank them dry. But everybody enjoyed it. And the crew either got back or were brought back in trucks, laid out by the ship and then the bosun and his mate would hose everybody down till they came round and were fit enough to go on board again. Well, that was the end of our stay in Sydney and the end of that voyage and as far as we were concerned, the end of the war. So, very nice.

DIASPORA

From the middle of the year 1945 it was as if the world was in the aftermath of some howling storm. Now the wind had died down and the floodwaters had receded, human flotsam and jetsam were to be found all across the world. As already mentioned, there were Americans and Australians in Europe or in the Pacific Islands who wanted to go home. There were Japanese, German and Italian prisoners in Canada and Australia desperate for repatriation. There were British and Australian prisoners in Japan and Germany even more desperate to return. There were British and Australian women who had married Americans yearning to see their husbands

and their new countries. And in Europe, hundreds of thousands of refugees, who were without any place to call home, were preparing to turn their backs on their own continent and seek a new life in the New World.

Even before the war in the Pacific had ended, a British general election had dismissed Churchill as Prime Minister and replaced him with Clement Attlee. Attlee had promised to get the troops home, and British voters had given him an overwhelming political victory. Now it was time to keep that promise. A week after the defeat of Japan, Attlee asked for his Cunard liners back, but Truman, who had succeeded Roosevelt as President of the United States, negotiated to keep the *Queen Mary* until all the GI brides had been ferried across the Atlantic. There were, after all, 25,000 of them, as well as 15,000 children.[19]

In the cold January of 1946 the *Queen Mary* started yet another refit. But not yet would her splendid pre-war luxury furnishings grace the great liner. This time the accommodation was designed for women and children. High

British warbrides leave for the USA in 1945. One of the last duties the liners performed before returning to peacetime duties was to ferry the wives and brides of allied troops to their new homelands in an operation aptly named 'Operation Diaper'.

chairs and playpens were found, and drying lines for nappies (soon the GI brides would be calling them diapers) were set up in the empty swimming pool. The American authorities, mindful of the responsibilities of motherhood, banned alcohol. On 5 February, the great liner sailed from England bound for the United States, carrying 1,706 brides and 604 children, most of them seasick. Captain Illingworth blamed British rationing. 'The poor dears had been starved for chocolate. When they found the canteens loaded with sweets, I'm afraid they overindulged.' Perhaps the Americans should have banned chocolate as well as alcohol!

In the first eighteen months after the end of the war, the *Queen Mary* carried 12,886 GI brides and their babies to America, and around another 10,000 to Canada. As if desperate to get back into peacetime service, she returned from Canada in her best time ever, 3 days, 22 hours and 42 minutes, at an average speed of 32 knots – and there were no U-boats to dodge.[20]

Plenty of GI brides sailed across the Pacific as well. The American troops who had arrived on the *Queen Mary* and other ships to help defend Australia had not spent all their time fighting. This time the transport would be in the ships of the Matson Line which, before the war, had been the stars of the California–Australia route. Launched in the early 1930s, the 'Matson Sisters', the *Mariposa, Monterey* and *Lurline* were very similar to each other, each about 18,000 tons. They had cut the running time on the route by a third, and were comfortable or, if the Matson publicity was to be believed, totally luxurious. 'They run the gamut of sumptuous living at sea . . . Ship life vibrant with the sorcery of the South Seas . . . Night club gaiety catching its glitter from the Southern Cross . . .' But by 1945 they had suffered a hard war, the *Monterey* in particular having a distinguished record of action as a troop-ship in the Mediterranean during the Allied invasion of Italy. There had not been a lot of opportunity to spruce her up for bridal transport.[21]

Betty Macallen travelled on the *Lurline* even before the war ended, when Japanese aircraft were still patrolling the Pacific:

One night at dinner after we arrived in San Francisco I said to two of the officers, 'Whatever happened one night? I heard those motors. They just seemed to have got so noisy.' He said, 'We can tell you now. You were fired at by Japs. But we couldn't tell you on board. Imagine having 200 women jump overboard.'

Some of the Australian girls who married American servicemen still meet regularly in the United States, where they still live. Linda Schwartz travelled on the *Monterey*. She recalls:

I was in a cabin with three other girls, and it was a section of the boat where there was a bathroom in the centre. One bathroom, but each cabin had a toilet in it. And the bathroom was so dirty that we used to stand in the toilet instead and we'd soap ourselves and the girls would rinse us off with the water, which was kind of salty water really. And I became quite sick on the boat. I didn't have too much time down in the dining-room. Actually I lost 32lb (16kg) on the trip. I had a great figure when I got off that boat.

Lorraine Zenchyk comes from Sydney. She remembers: It was the *Monterey*. Previously it was a luxury liner, but it had been through the war, still had its camouflage colours on it and everything like that. And the food, they had so much food for us, you know, it was just really great.' Kathleen Lions agrees: 'Well, the food was very good. Everything was excellent . . . the crew were very good, I can't say anything bad about the ship, it was lovely.'

On board the *Lurline* to San Francisco, Margery Sciapa shared the ship with 4,000 soldiers, and remembers leaving Brisbane:

When the ship first moved off I felt so excited to be on a ship that was actually moving. All the fellas were up on the wharves, the roofs, and they were yelling out, 'You'll be sorry'. And I remember they blew the ship's whistle and every little baby within 40 miles (60km) started screaming its head off. But it was exciting. Everything was new and different, and I remember seeing the flying fish and thinking 'how wonderful'. And looking behind and seeing the wake of the boat and thinking . . . it takes a long time before it disappears.

After repatriation and GI brides came immigrants. For many years, until the era of cheap air travel, the shipping lines made a substantial and consistent profit from transporting the migrants now leaving Europe in scores of thousands.

The most famous of the lines away from the North Atlantic, the P&O, rapidly restored their services to the East and to Australia. The officers and men who had sailed the liners as troop-ships during the war were joined by the young post-war recruits who were destined for rapid promotion as the lines expanded. Dennis Scott-Masson had qualified as a navigator for P&O by the age of twenty-two, and remembers his years aboard some of P&O's less fancy migrant passenger ships in the late Forties and Fifties:

> After the war, some of our older ships were converted to carry migrants only. There were no full-fare paying passengers as such. One of these ships was the *Ranchi*. We carried about 900 migrants from Britain to Australia in her. These voyages were completely subsidized by the Australian government so the shipping company made a nice profit. I remember one voyage when we had virtually all Irish migrants going out to Australia. They were, shall we say, a fairly rough bunch. They were cutting off their roots, and so they were sceptical about the future. They didn't know what they were going to. Some of them didn't even know which city in Australia they would end up in.
>
> When we sailed from Tilbury on these voyages, there were very few family members or friends at the quayside. The farewells had been made at home. The migrants came down by train to the ship. So it wasn't actually a very fond farewell at the ship as they left British soil, sometimes for ever. The voyages themselves could be unpleasant. I recall one trip on the old *Ranchi*. Her engines were no longer reliable. Somewhere, soon after we left Port Said and entered the canal, we broke down completely. We were immovable. We had to drop anchor in the canal and tie up alongside the bank. No ship could go north or south. I believe we held up a record number of ships, eighty-two in all, until we were finally towed out of the canal into Suez Bay. And that was a voyage with a full load of 900 migrants on that non-air-conditioned ship. They weren't happy.

The Australian Minister for Immigration, Arthur Calwell, knew that his country desperately needed the migrants. 'I am going abroad to seek ships for immigrants,' he said. 'If we have no ships we shall get no immigrants. And without immigrants the future of the Australia we know will be both uneasy and brief. As a nation we shall not survive. Give me the ships and I will guarantee to load them with the right type of our future Australians.'

Increasing numbers of shipowners began to see a future in the movement of migrants to Australia. Britain's Shaw Savill Line, primarily with their 20,200-ton *Southern Cross*, the first major liner to mount her engines and therefore her funnel aft (in 1955), and her near-sister *Northern Star*, worked a 76-day around-the-world schedule that included calls at Fremantle, Melbourne, Sydney and Wellington. Another British firm, the New Zealand Shipping Company, ran several very large combination passenger-cargo ships out from London to Auckland and Wellington, using the Panama route in both directions. Such ships derived considerable incomes from the meat and wool trades. The Italians and the Greeks also invested strongly. Companies such as the Flotto Lauro, Sitmar, Cogedar and the Chandris Lines took second-hand ships, rebuilt them and in the process usually doubled their original capacities, often with six- and eight-berth cabins. Homebound, these ships carried budget tourists bound for holidays in Britain or in Europe, and young Australians seeking their fortunes in the Old World, or enlarging their experience and qualifications. It was on these Europe-bound journeys that the lines made handsome profits, while the migrant trade was their bread and butter.

Captain Adriano Borreani of the *Achille Lauro* saw the migration at its height:

> On our outbound Australian trips, we were always packed until the early 1970s, sometimes with a capacity 1,735 on board. There were British mostly in first class and then all the mixed nationalities in tourist class. Many of these migrants had their fares paid for them under the Australian resettlement programme. Many had no luggage. Some were pregnant, even past three months. Once, a Lebanese couple had their baby on board. She was named Laura after *Lauro*.

The Shaw Saville Line's 20,000-ton *Southern Cross*, built by Harland & Wolff in Belfast in 1955, was the first modern liner to mount the funnel at the rear.

On 16 June 1946, the *Queen Elizabeth* was returned to Cunard and the mammoth task of restoration began.

He adds:

> The summer trips in June, July and August were the most trying. The Indian Ocean monsoons caused a great deal of seasickness. Many passengers were petrified and it was impossible to persuade them to leave their cabins, and we had so many languages, it was impossible to communicate. With the Yugoslavians in particular, we had to use hand-language. But when these passengers were well, they ate anything and everything. If one of them died on board, we usually buried them at sea, especially since the family had no money. We always did this at 2am, without the other passengers seeing it.

The last Australian government fare-assisted migrant contract for sea travel was given to the Greek Chandris Lines. 'Our migrant passengers,' says Chandris Captain Nickos Volovinos, 'often travelled with great trunks, which they visited in the baggage rooms or in the holds during the voyage. Often, they changed from northern winter to southern summer clothing in the midst of the four-week voyage. There was an English teacher on board, provided by the Australian government.' Chandris had the Australian government's migrant contract for nearly ten years, from 1968 until 1977. If a migrant's application was accepted, it meant a fare of £10 for the trip. Some passengers travelled with cases filled with nothing more than Greek olive oil; others so feared the sea that they never left their cabins.

Captain John Tourvas adds:

> Chandris at its peak delivered 50,000 Europeans a year to Australia. Our ships were always full up. At peak, we used five liners with a total of 7,000 berths. The *Australis* [launched in 1939 as the *America*] was our premier and fastest ship. She was routed from Bremerhaven, Rotterdam and Southampton to Las Palmas, Cape Town and then over to Fremantle, Melbourne and Sydney. She then continued to Auckland and then homewards via Suva, sometimes Los Angeles, Acapulco, the Panama Canal, Port Everglades, sometimes the Azores and finally back to Southampton. We were scheduled for twenty-eight days from Southampton to Sydney.

It had taken about the same time for the early European migrants to cross the Atlantic to the promised land of America. Two million people sailed halfway around the world in this new migration.

Soon there would be more people on the move, but this time not out of grim necessity. As the decade of the 1950s dawned, American money from the Marshall Plan was helping to rebuild western Europe and bring about a previously unheard-of prosperity. Travel for business and travel for pleasure began to become not only possible but affordable again, and the great liners were repainted and repolished until they shone in the sunlight of a new day.

THE LAST HURRAH

While the *Queen Mary* was ferrying GI brides to the United States during 1946, the *Queen Elizabeth* was in dry dock at Southampton. Her grey wartime overcoat was chipped off, and she emerged gloriously again in the company colours, red and black funnels, white topsides and black hull – 30 tons of paint in all.[22] Then *Queen Mary* returned, and it was her turn to have the scars of war – initials carved on handrails, hobnail marks on decks, painted icons and slogans everywhere – removed. French polishers french-polished, upholsterers upholstered, painters painted, and removal men laboured to return the sofas, carpets, curtains and mattresses that had been in store since the outbreak of war.

As the time for her maiden civilian voyage drew near, the supplies for her passengers were carried on board the *Queen Elizabeth*. While the citizens of Southampton made do with the post-war ration of a few ounces (grams) of meat or cheese, a little sugar, some whale meat and as many potatoes as they could grow in the backyard, they must have been astonished to read the menu for the maiden voyage:

GRAPEFRUIT AU KIRSCH
HORS-D'ŒUVRES VARIÉS
SOUP: CONSOMMÉ ROYALE, CREAM OF MUSHROOM
FISH: RED MULLET MEUNIÈRE, HALIBUT SAUCE MOUSSELINE
ENTRÉES: CROQUETTE OF DUCKLING, TÊTE DE VEAU VINAIGRETTE
JOINT: LEG AND SHOULDER OF LAMB WITH MINT SAUCE
VEGETABLES: GREEN PEAS, CAULIFLOWER

And so on. They were all, so Cunard assured the public, purchased in the United States or Canada where such delights were freely obtainable.[23] The *Queen Elizabeth*'s long-delayed maiden voyage in peacetime took place in October 1946.

On 31 July 1947 *Queen Mary* sailed from Southampton to inaugurate Cunard's two-liner weekly service; the very next day, *Queen Elizabeth* sailed from New York. There had been some changes. Ballrooms had become cinemas, and there were new murals in the public rooms: 'Gay, vivid compositions with mermaids in scarlet jackets and underwater revelry in the realms of Neptune.' Even the crew's quarters were updated and improved.[24]

The *Queen Mary* carried 701 passengers in first class, 478 in cabin class and 725 in third class, the *Queen Elizabeth* a total of about a 100 more. For years, they were almost always full, and delivering handsome profits to Cunard. The service remained matchless: for breakfast, a choice of 11 different cereals, 5 sorts of toast and 80 cooked dishes whiled

away the morning for passengers waiting for a 5-course lunch.

Now, finally, Cunard had its intended two-ship relay, originally planned in 1926, between Southampton and New York with a call at Cherbourg in each direction.[25] Michael Dodds, a Cunard captain, recalls:

> We went backwards and forwards, and everybody enjoyed it. The food was out of this world, especially compared to those post-war years in Britain. We had great entertainment on board as well. And for the passengers, we had all the names you could think of. In the first-class dining saloon, we always saw a great number of celebrities. And we also had quite a lot of Church people travelling during those years. I remember enjoying a chat with the Archbishop of Canterbury. And we had members of the Royal Family. Queen Elizabeth the Queen Mother travelled with us in 1954. I was with her party when the ship, the *Queen Elizabeth*, was rolling in very bad weather. I remember saying, 'Ma'am, I think you had better take your shoes off and, I think, sit down before you fall because the ship takes violent rolls.' Anyway, she did just that with a little smile. She took her shoes off. I looked after them and finally put them back on her feet at the end of the party. She was very pleasant. When we finally reached the Hudson River, there was an enormous welcome. They all knew the Queen Mother. I remember one of the ferries travelling between Manhattan and New Jersey was called *Elizabeth* and this caught her eye. All the ships were blowing and the sirens were going. I showed the Queen Mother the bridge and the port around us. She was delighted at the welcome she was being given by the port of New York.

Captain Dodds adds:

> New York Harbor was a very exciting place in those days. I used to travel around the port by tug, going from pier to pier, from ship to ship, as a Cunard superintendent. I looked after the Cunard cargo fleet as well. But the most impressive occasions were the arrivals of the big passenger liners. It was always a sight to behold. The passengers all went to one side as you passed the Statue of Liberty, and then the other side to watch the tip of Manhattan and to follow all the piers along the Hudson River. Working for Cunard then was like working for a national institution. The British were very proud of Cunard. Occasionally, we had problems such as dockers' strikes. We had to tie up big liners like the *Queen Mary* and *Queen Elizabeth* ourselves. We would have to rig the rigging for the gangways and then take the baggage off ourselves, load the mail, discharge mail, and all the work. We didn't go home at these times. We slept there, either on the ship or on the pier itself, and we'd get $20 a day extra.

Everett Viez was a regular Cunard Atlantic passenger in the 1950s and sailed on most of their passenger ships. He recalls:

> Cunard was a wonderful company in those days, filled with all the traditions of the great ocean liners. The *Queen Mary* was my absolute favourite. She was top-notch. The *Queen Elizabeth*, rather oddly, never quite had the same personality. I remember when we boarded the *Mary* on a cold, windy night at Cherbourg in October 1956. The winds delayed her. She couldn't dock. So we boarded by tender, at 11.30pm, in the cold darkness. But Cunard service was impeccable. We were escorted to our cabin with the electric fireplace already working. A full dinner was served at midnight, ending at a quarter to two in the morning. On the five-day crossing over to New York, the ship was absolutely perfect.

John Dempsey was masseur on the *Queen Elizabeth* in the golden post-war years:

> The *Queen Elizabeth* was my home. There were times when I used to join the ship in Southampton, go up the gangway, go down to my room, sort out the locker and all that stuff, and go and have a pint at the Pig and Whistle [the traditional name for the ship's bar], go along to my swimming pool and Turkish bath and massage, open the door, look in and say, 'Who have we got today? Oh, yeah, we've got Lord Beaverbrook, Duke of Windsor, I see David Niven's coming in today', and we'd book them. Ladies were between 10am and 2pm, gentlemen from 2 to 7pm. Then you had your dinner, had a pint of beer and go to bed. And I'd realize when we got to New York I hadn't seen the sky in five days.

For the crew, not all the passengers were good news. John Minto was a waiter on Cunarders:

> And you only got one tip, if you ever got it at all, sometimes. I

always remember a lady gave me 2s 6d, 2s 6d now is worth 12½p (20 cents). She gave me this half a crown for looking after her for five days. And as she got up and gave me the money, I said, 'No, you better keep it. You'd need it more than I do.' And I gave her another half a crown so she could get a taxi.

The post-war Cunard slogan was 'Getting there is half the fun' and at that time the North Atlantic seemed to belong to Cunard. They were the biggest, the best-known and, in some ways, the best-run Atlantic shipping company. In 1957, they had the 'largest fleet on the Atlantic' with no less than twelve

passenger ships – the giant *Queen Elizabeth* and *Queen Mary*, the *Mauretania, Caronia, Britannic*, the combination passenger-cargo liners *Media* and *Parthia*, the pre-war veteran *Scythia* and, finally, four brand-new vessels, the sister ships *Saxonia, Ivernia, Carinthia* and *Sylvania*. In peak summers, there might be as many as four sailings a week from New York, bound for ports such as Cherbourg, Le Havre, Cobh, Southampton or Liverpool.

Curiously, as they were scarcely involved in the pre-war years, it was the Americans who produced the most noteworthy Atlantic 'superliner' of the post-war era. She was

'Getting there is half the fun' was Cunard's very apt slogan for 1950s Atlantic travel. Splendour and majesty are evident in this view of the *Queen Mary*'s first-class Main Lounge.

In the 1950s, sailing day was an event. If 2,000 passengers were sailing for Europe as many as 5,000 family, friends and visitors came down to see them off.

the exceptional *United States*. Previously, the United States Lines seemed content with more medium-sized ships (with the obvious exception of the giant *Leviathan* in the 1920s and early 1930s, which had been a German ship, handed over in war reparations in 1919, and previously the *Vaterland* of 1914). The decision to build a brand-new American 'supership' was actually sparked off by two considerations: potential from commercial profit on a booming North Atlantic trade route and, perhaps more importantly, the possible need for another wartime troop-ship (the Korean War had begun as she was being built and the Cold War constantly threatened a possible World War III). The military interest in the construction of the *United States* was a result of the great success of the two Cunard *Queen*s as wartime troopers. Now military sponsors in Washington wanted a potential troop-ship of their own and so, in a joint effort with United States Lines, underwrote what would become the most technologically advanced 'superliner' of her day. In fact, the US government would pay for nearly 70 percent of the ship's exceptional $78 million cost.

The Pentagon insisted on three prime ingredients for the new 'supership': extraordinary safety, amazing speed and, of course, quick and easy convertibility into a military troop-ship. No ship was more fireproof. Her designer, William Francis Gibbs, insisted on lightweight construction. More aluminium was used in her than in any other vessel afloat, even wooden picture frames not being permitted on board. It was said that the only wood on board the *United States* was in the butcher's block and the piano. Actually, Gibbs had rigorously argued with the Steinway Company to get them to produce an aluminium piano and Steinway firmly refused. The ship was 990ft (270m) long, almost as long as the *Queen*s, but her lightweight build kept her gross weight to 30,000 tons less.[26]

The *United States* was the last liner to win the Blue Riband. Her actual top speed, like most of her special design components, was kept a secret for some years after her completion. It was eventually revealed that for a short time during her sea trials, in June 1952, she managed 38.25 knots, with her four sets of Westinghouse turbines generating 240,000hp, almost 100,000 more than her nearest rival. At one brief point, she climbed to 43 knots and then did as much as 20 knots in reverse. In July of 1952, she took the Blue Riband from the *Queen Mary* with ease. The new liner's speed was recorded at 35.59 knots, and she bettered the *Queen Mary*'s time by 10 hours and 2 minutes. And so the honours went to a ship flying the Stars and Stripes for the first time since the old Collins Line a century before.

The 990ft-long *United States* received a gala welcome along the Hudson River on her first visit to New York in June 1952.

Germany's pre-war *Europa* was given to the French as reparations and, beginning in 1950, reappeared on the Atlantic as the restyled *Liberté*.

During the post-war boom there seemed to be less need, also, for the nationalistic fervour of the 1930s. There was business for all, and old rivalries were put to one side while the shipping lines prospered. Even the French were somewhat less flamboyant. Their only pre-war survivor, the superb *Ile de France*, was joined by a former German ship, the celebrated record-breaker *Europa*, which came to France as reparation after the war and was restyled by 1950 as the *Liberté*. But the French Line rekindled much of its splendid pre-war reputation, deserved not only for their spectacular cuisine, but for their meticulous service and luxurious first-class accommodation. No steamer company, transatlantic or otherwise, had more red-suited bell-boys, glistening champagne buckets, fresh flowers in Lalique vases and onion soup on the breakfast menu. *New York Times* writer Ada Louise Huxtable wrote years later, in 1980, 'The French Line had only one standard – the superlative. In the realm of the sybaritic, the French always seemed to do it best. Until its very last days, their liners were considered the best French restaurants in the world. The vin ordinaire was free, the cellars a hushed treasury of rare vintages and the chefs leaped to anticipate the most epicurean demand.'

The *Ile de France*, having resumed luxury service in 1949, returned with almost the same decorative style that had made her such a favourite in the Thirties and with her three funnels reduced to a more stylish two. She was redecorated in a late version of Art Deco, incorporating some pieces from the magnificent *Normandie*. The *Liberté* (formerly *Europa*) was the perfect complement to the celebrated *Ile de France*. There were more touches of latter-day Art Deco, some streamlining and softening of the severely geometric Teutonic decor, more pieces from the *Normandie* and, of course, a superb restaurant.

The Dutch, remaining quite conservative in nature until the mid-1950s, then added two passenger ships in 1951–52 that would revolutionize the marketing philosophy of the North Atlantic passage. The 15,000-ton sister ships *Ryndam* and *Maasdam*, originally intended to be 60-passenger combination passenger-cargo ships, were redesigned in the earliest stages of construction and became 900-passenger 'tourist ships'. Carrying a mere 39 first-class travellers in very élite quarters, the 850 or so in tourist class occupied an unparalleled 90 per cent of the ship's accommodation. Furthermore, it was the most comfortable tourist space of the day: a string of pleasant public rooms, a full restaurant, spacious outer decks and even an open-air swimming pool. With fares offered for as little as £7 ($20) a day (8 days from New to Cobh, 9 days to Southampton and Le Havre, and 8 days to Rotterdam), the significance of these ships cannot be overestimated. Tourist-class dominance of accommodation soon spread to every new Atlantic liner. As first and cabin-class travellers began to desert ships for aeroplanes, the bulk of the remaining trade, at least into the early 1960s, was the tourist-class passenger.

In time, the other lines were tempted into building for prestige again. A big liner offered a sort of travelling trade fair, demonstrating the best in technology, fashion, craftsmanship and sheer style for nations anxious to sell their wares overseas. There was even the possibility of profitable operation. The Italians began their rebuilding in the early 1950s, first for the South American trade and then, in 1953–54, for the more luxurious run to New York. While they had sailed the giant *Rex* and *Conte di Savoia* in the pre-war years, the directors in Genoa now saw the huge 'superliners' as bygone symbols of a seemingly lost age, dinosaurs of the oceans. Consequently, their new transatlantic flagships were the smaller 29,000-ton sister ships *Andrea Doria* and *Cristoforo Colombo*. The West Germans, still caught in the

restrictions of post-war control, added their first passenger ship, the elderly *Gripsholm* of 1925, which began sailing as the *Berlin* in 1955. The Swedes and the Norwegians, among the more seriously interested in a balanced passenger/touring trade of nine or so months on the Atlantic and the rest in warm-weather cruising, opted for some of the more contemporary styles of marine design. The *Kungsholm* of 1953, for example, was the first North Atlantic liner to have all outside state-rooms (like the 'Strength through Joy' ship *Wilhelm Gustloff*) while the *Bergensfjord* of 1956, like the *United States*, made extensive use of aluminium in her construction. They were portents of things to come.

For the time being, the 'superliners' and their smaller sisters sailed on. Among those first-class lounges, salons and suites came world celebrities. The most photographed were the Duke and Duchess of Windsor. They rarely travelled with fewer than ninety-five pieces of luggage via Cunard, until that company indicated politely but firmly that they were no longer prepared to put up with their massively expensive requirements, so subsequently they 'chose' the *United States* to travel on. Hollywood stars had their favourite liners. Marlene Dietrich crossed on the *Queen Elizabeth* and the *Normandie*, Elizabeth Taylor on the *Queen Mary* while Lana Turner preferred the more club-like surroundings of the *Mauretania*. Then there were figures from politics such as Winston Churchill, Dwight Eisenhower, President Tito of Yugoslavia, Queen Frederika of Greece and the Crown Prince of Norway. Reporters customarily met the inward bound ships in New York's Lower Bay or immediately upon docking. They would go aboard and have several hours to interview and photograph the more famous passengers. But once, hearing that a small army of reporters awaited her disembarkation, secretive film star Greta Garbo left the *Queen Mary* disguised as a Cunard stewardess via the lower-deck crew gangway.

The technological imperative of warfare had also caused a huge improvement in passenger aeroplanes. Skills that had been learned in designing and constructing the great US bombers were turned after the war to building airliners: Stratocruisers and Constellations began to ply the passenger

routes, and, by 1953, 38 percent of transatlantic passengers travelled by air. This time, the United States took a lead that she had never possessed on the seas. (Britain had the first jet airliner, the Comet, but a number of disastrous crashes ended that pioneer effort.) In October 1958, a mere six years after the *United States* was first commissioned and captured the Blue Riband, the early Boeing 707s began a regular commercial jet service on the North Atlantic. Suddenly and abruptly, transatlantic travel time became six hours instead of four days. The difference was irresistible. Within six months, the airlines secured two-thirds of all Atlantic travel. By 1965, they had 95 per cent. Consequently, the 1960s were largely years of decline and withdrawal for transatlantic passenger shipowners. Winter crossings dwindled to a very few, fleets were reduced, staffs cut and, in the end, those vast, ornate lounges and orderly promenades had grown very desolate. Many directors of steamship lines in their mahogany-panelled boardrooms at first ignored these airline competitors. One director at Cunard responded in October 1958, 'Flying is but a fad. There will always be passengers to fill ships like the *Queen*s.' But even that illustrious pair fell on hard times. On one crossing, the *Queen Elizabeth* arrived with 200 passengers being looked after by 1,200 crew. It was an unsustainable proposition.

In *The Sway of the Grand Saloon* (Arlington Books, 1986), John Malcolm Brinnin wrote that a single passenger might:

> . . . turn up for tea in the dim depths of the Grand Saloon and sit, magnificently alone, while a dozen white-jacketed stewards stood about like sentries, alert to his command. As he chose his sandwiches and scones and cakes from portable caddies, as all the pyramidal napkins on all the white tables in the gloaming multiplied his sense of isolation, he might note that a shadowy figure at the furthest end of the room was seating himself at the Wurlitzer. Then, as the great ship creaked and rolled, the intruder would shiver the air with selections from 'Rose Marie' and 'The Desert Song'.

For the Cunard line it seemed that the song of success might have ended after over a hundred years of service on the North Atlantic.

NOTES

1 Robert Lacey, *The Queens of the Atlantic*, Sidgwick & Jackson, 1973, page 68.

2 *Ibid*.

3 *Ibid*.

4 Lacey, *op.cit.*, page 67.

5. Quoted in Maddocks, *op cit.*

6. Quoted in Maddocks, *op cit.*

7 Lacey, *op.cit.*, page 74.

8 Lacey, *op.cit.*, page 75.

9 Lacey, *op.cit.*, page 80.

10 Maddocks, *op cit.*, page 150.

11 Lacey, *op.cit.*, page 84.

12 Maddocks, *op cit.*, page 154.

13 Maddocks, *op cit.*, page 154.

14 Bob Wall, *Ocean Liners*, Collins, 1978, page 232.

15 Maddocks, *op cit.*, page 147.

16 Maddocks, *op cit.*, page 112.

17 Maddocks, *op cit.*, page 112.

18 In the film *Der Fell Cap Arcona*.

19 Lacey, *op.cit.*, page 96.

20 Maddocks, *op cit.*, page 155.

21 Frank Braynard, Willa Braynard and William H. Miller, Stephens, 1987, *50 Famous Liners*, Stephens, 1987, pages 141–5.

22 Lacey, *op.cit.*, page 100.

23 Lacey, *op.cit.*, page 100.

24 Lacey, *op.cit.*, page 101.

25 Lacey, *op.cit.*, page 36.

26 Bob Wall, *Ocean Liners*, Collins, 1978, page 207.

OPPOSITE:
Marlene Dietrich is photographed amidst a collection of her trunks and cases aboard the *Normandie* in 1938.

BELOW:
Greta Garbo boarding the *Queen Mary* in Southampton in 1947.

CHAPTER FOUR

THE
WORLD TOUR

When national pride is aroused, emotions tend to take over from reason. Though the Second World War might have been expected to cure Europe of nationalism for ever, it showed again after the war in the transatlantic race for supremacy. Certainly, in spite of the rapid exodus of paying passengers to the new airliners, the western European nations began once again to build those luxurious symbols of national pride, the ocean liners.

TWILIGHT'S LAST GLEAMING:
THE WHITE ELEPHANTS

Soon after the Second World War the last great blue-water passenger ship services had begun to reopen. These routes went out to South America, South Africa, the Middle East, Australia and the Orient. The P&O Lines, also known as the P&O-Orient Lines from 1960 until 1966, after its merger with the Orient Line, had the biggest and most important long-distance liner fleet in the post-war years. In fact, by 1960, P&O-Orient had the largest liner fleet anywhere, even surpassing the Cunard Company. P&O was best known after the Second World War for their service out to Australia, to Fremantle, Melbourne and Sydney. Their well-known Indian service, to Bombay, declined considerably after 1947, when India became an independent nation.

After wartime losses and then the prospect of profitable days ahead, both the P&O and the Orient Lines had embarked, soon after 1945, on a huge rebuilding programme. No fewer than seven major liners were built between 1948 and 1954. The Orient Line added three ships, the 1,545-passenger *Orcades* of 1948, the *Oronsay* of 1951 and then the *Orsova* of 1954. They were among the most modern-looking liners of their time. The P&O Lines, having had great success with their five *Strath* liners from the 1930s, copied their basic design, with some refinements, in the 27,900-ton, 1,159-passenger *Himalaya* of 1949, the *Chusan* of 1950 and, finally, a pair of

OPPOSITE:
P&O's most luxurious liner to date, the *Royal Princess*: designed for North American cruises including regular trips to the Alaskan glacier area.

near-sisters, the *Arcadia* and *Iberia* of 1954.

P&O Captain Dennis Scott-Masson notes:

We still had strong links to India after the war. We still had the tea planters and the civil servants who ran India and who went out for considerable periods of time. They always went home to Britain for their leaves. And of course their wives and families travelled with them by sea. They were a very élite group of people. And of course they got to know their favourite ships and we got to know them very well.

P&O also catered for a first-class clientele on the Australian run. Captain Scott-Masson adds:

I remember one well-known family from southern Australia. They loved our *Arcadia*. They had special furniture built to order to fit in several of her deluxe cabins. On their annual pilgrimages to and from Britain, they had it installed in these rooms for their personal use. They arrived in Britain at the beginning of the summer, so they had the best of the weather, and then left in early autumn to return to Australia.

Even in the mid-1950s, as the North Atlantic trade began to shudder under the thunderous sounds of aero-engines, the P&O-Orient Australian route seemed to have a very promising future, which led to an order for the two biggest and fastest liners ever built for a service other than on the North Atlantic. The Orient liner was the 41,900-ton *Oriana*, the fastest ship ever to sail to Sydney, making the passage from Southampton via Suez in twenty-one days flat. It was said that she was the first British liner that could seriously substitute for one of the 28½-knot Cunard *Queen*s on the Southampton–New York express run. The second new giant came several months later from the illustrious Harland & Wolff yards at Belfast, which had produced the *Olympic, Titanic* and dozens of other passenger ships. Named *Canberra*, she reached 45,700 tons and could carry as many as 2,272 passengers (her capacity was even greater than that of the world's largest liner, the *Queen Elizabeth*, which had a capacity of 2,223).

Had they been superstitious, the boards of directors of the great national lines might have paused to consider the events of the night of 25 July 1956. By this time, ships had sophisticated communications systems, and shipborne radar enabled them virtually to see in the dark – or in fog. Yet with all this in place, two modern ships captained by two experienced seamen collided only a few miles from the Nantucket lightship on the American east coast.

The *Andrea Doria* was an Italian liner of 29,100 tons, bound for New York in thick fog. The smaller Swedish *Stockholm* was on her way home to Europe, and only a few miles from the Italian ship. Still in clear weather, she was unable to see that she was nearing a fog-bank that hid a huge liner. At 11.09pm, the *Stockholm* struck the *Andrea Doria* with her specially strengthened steel bow and opened a 40-ft (12-m) gash in her. The water rushed in, overwhelming the protective watertight compartments and, like the *Titanic* before her, the *Andrea Doria* was doomed. Forty-four people on board perished, and five on the *Stockholm*. By chance, the old *Ile de France* was nearby, and answered the two liners' calls for help. French broadcaster/journalist Claude Villers recalls the event: 'All at once the captain of *Ile de France*

came up with the idea to turn on all the lights of his vessel, and in the fog those who had escaped from the *Andrea Doria* said later that they saw it light up all at once in the middle of the night . . . and the liner was awarded the *Légion d'Honneur*.' Perhaps it was the memory of that much-loved old ship that at least partly prompted France into extending her presence on the Atlantic by building another large, expensive liner.

The 66,300-ton *France* was the final 'superliner' built solely for Atlantic service. She received one of New York's last gala welcomes, in February 1962: tugs, spraying fireboats, ferries and overhead aircraft. But, as French historian Daniel Hillon says: 'This liner was launched the year of the opening of the first aerial connection between Paris and New York. But the liner didn't serve its purpose because it was born at the wrong time. A liner born dead.'

The *France* took 4 years, 3 months and 28 days to complete, in the same dockyard where the first *France*, the *Ile de France* and the *Normandie* were constructed. Jean-Paul Herbert, the French Line historian:

> At the time we had *Ile de France*. She was built in 1927, so I would not say she was derelict, but old-fashioned and over twenty-five years old after the war. We also had *Liberté*, she was *Europa* in the Thirties, so she was also twenty-five years of age. So we had to renew. France was not a wealthy country at the time, we had many problems. We had to rebuild the country itself, not just the ships.

Initial studies had suggested that one 66,000-tonner was superior to a pair of 30,000-tonners, and the notion of one great ship had a certain appeal as a statement of national confidence. The new ship was accordingly underwritten by the government of President de Gaulle. The *France*'s capacity was sensibly divided between 500 in first class and 1,500 in tourist, and her overall design of 1,035ft (310.5m) in length made her the longest liner ever built – 4ft (1.2m) longer than the *Queen Elizabeth* and 7ft (2.1m) beyond the *Normandie*.

Like most 'superliners' before her, the *France* was intended to dazzle the public. There was a splendid array of suites in first class, some with private decks and dining-rooms. Kennels on the sun deck had twenty separate compartments, all of them carpeted, and their comfort stations catered for both American and French dogs and therefore included a New York City fire hydrant and a Parisian lamp-post.

Claude Villers often travelled aboard the *France*:

> The shape, on the horizon, on the ocean, made quite a picture. The design with both its funnels and its masts was superb – but on the interior it was one of the first vessels not to have wood, which made it quite cold-looking. But there was a possibility to eat and drink all day long, all night if you wanted . . . it's fantastic, it's a society that moves around in time and space. Whether people love or hate one another, all is possible on a liner, like in any city.

Villers was often able to travel first class as a perk of his job. 'It was the discovery of a whole new world, one that we don't even imagine when we travel in the inferior classes. You order in the middle of the Atlantic Ocean any meal you liked and the chef would endeavour to prepare it for you.'

France was not the only European nation hungry for *grandeur*. No country expended more lavishly on the post-war liners than Italy, already rivalling France as the home of style, chic and luxury. In the *dolce vita* years of Italy's post-war boom, the future seemed positive when the magnificent *Leonardo da Vinci*, a 33,300-tonner, was commissioned in 1960, as if to expunge the disaster of the *Andrea Doria*. But in 1965, three years after the *France* was commissioned, the Italian Line misguidedly added not one but two 'superliners' for its express service to New York. The first was the 45,900-ton *Michelangelo*, which was introduced in the spring of 1965; her sister ship, the *Raffaello*, followed in the summer. The two ships represented a total investment by the Italian government of $120 million.

The new, all-white twins boasted unusual profiles. In keeping with a growing trend, the two funnels were placed well aft, making room for an extensive first-class pool and lido section. However, every cabin in all three classes had private facilities. Each ship had six swimming pools, three for the adults and the others for children, the three largest pools

heated by infrared for use on chilly days.

The gorgeous Italian ships were far too late. Perhaps they served to represent the best of Italian design to the world, and they thus earned their keep indirectly, but maybe the Italian government should have invested its money elsewhere. The trip from Italy via Nice and Gibraltar was much longer than the trip from Cherbourg or Southampton, and becoming less attractive. But economic realities were a minor consideration. Their construction had been pushed on by the powerful Italian labour unions as well as national pride, and neither ship ever earned a single lira.

By 1960, all of the post-war liners were given complete air conditioning and better entertainment facilities. Like the Atlantic liner companies, P&O began to recognize that the liners had to be more than just transport, that they were moving resorts that had to provide more and more recreation.

The P&O passenger fleet was first affected by airline competition in the late 1960s. Responding to the first challenge, one company captain recalled, 'We sent our liners on longer and more diverse sailings, roaming the world looking for passengers to fill our increasingly empty berths.' Faster, more efficient container ships began to take passenger-ship cargoes, then inexpensive charter flights lured away the budget tourist and migrant trades, and finally, as the ships grew older, they needed costly refits to meet new safety, regulatory and insurance standards. The end was inevitable. The P&O-Orient liners, like a parade of dying elephants, sailed off to the boneyards of Taiwan. Professor Tony Slaven:

> The Boeing 707 is one that really did the damage. Instead of taking thirty days to travel from London to Sydney, you could do it in thirty hours, more or less. You were very tired and you couldn't relax on the journey, but you could do it that way. I think everyone was surprised how quickly passenger preference shifted from those leisurely four-week journeys to the Antipodes to the one-day-and-a-half air journeys. In a rapidly expanding world economy, time became money. And so the liner trades collapsed dramatically and quickly.

Second to the mighty P&O passenger fleet in size, the Union Castle Line ran their mail liners on the express route from

Southampton to ports such as Cape Town, Port Elizabeth, East London and Durban. It was considered the world's most precise passenger service, sailing every Thursday from the Southampton docks at the stroke of four in the afternoon. 'We always sailed at exactly four o'clock on Thursdays, even if we only moved 2ft (60m) off the quay,' recalls Edna Dodds, a Union Castle nursing sister in the 1950s. 'They used to get their time clock set in Southampton on the first whistle as we moved out. And then, we docked six weeks later, after a round trip to South Africa, at six o'clock on a Friday morning. They were wonderful voyages.'

The 'Cape Mail Express' fleet in 1960 numbered eight major liners, the smallest of which was 20,000 tons. In the early Sixties, as the airlines took away their passengers, the Union Castle fleet would be reduced to five liners, including the brand-new, 37,600-ton *Windsor Castle* and the *Transvaal Castle*. The next step was delayed but inevitable. The Castle liners made their last voyage in the autumn of 1977.

In the early 1960s, Cunard directors, as always conservative and traditional, decided to replace the 25-year-old *Queen Mary*. They envisioned a liner that would retain the traditional three classes and work in tandem with *Queen Elizabeth*. This new design was codenamed 'Q3', the third *Queen*. But the era of the three-class ship was past, and there was no further need for two big Cunard liners in regular Atlantic relay. The design was abandoned in favour of a compromise to please an emerging new market that wanted warm-water cruises as well as the old market for the traditional ocean 'greyhound'.

The new 'superliner', 'Q4', was a blending of Atlantic liner and leisure cruise-ship. The new transatlantic passengers wanted shopping arcades, discos and Las Vegas-style shows in rooms that were now trimmed in stainless steel and formica rather than walnut and tapestry. There would only be two classes, first and tourist, and the class distinctions would be far less noticeable.

The first keel plates were laid down at the John Brown shipyards on Clydebank that had produced the previous *Queen*s, in June 1965. This time the atmosphere was subtly different from the pre-war euphoria, as one-time Clydebank worker, Tom McKendrick, recalls: 'The good times were coming, yes there was going to be employment. But it was only going to be short-term. It's not exactly jubilation, you know, but by the same token it's not exactly doom and despondency.' Certainly the externals were changing. The Cunard red and black funnel colours were to disappear. Indeed, there would be no funnels, only a vertical exhaust at the rear of the ship. The company had decided that it wanted a new image. On 20 September 1967, two days before the old *Queen Mary* was to leave New York on her very last Atlantic crossing, the Queen named the new ship after herself, *Queen Elizabeth II*.

The *QE2*, as she was soon nicknamed, left in November 1968 for her first sea trials, but then quickly encountered serious turbine problems. Humiliated, she crept back to the John Brown shipyards. Cunard refused delivery. Repaired, she finally put into Southampton, her home port, just after the New Year holidays. Now even more problems were uncovered, and once again Cunard refused their $80-million, 65,800-ton ship. There had been so much demand for berths on the maiden voyage that Cunard divided it into five separate voyages, but those celebratory maiden voyages had to be cancelled, costing over $10 million. *QE2* did not officially join the Cunard fleet until mid-April and the maiden trip, rescheduled as a direct Southampton–New York voyage, took place a month later.

In retrospect, the troubles surrounded the *QE2* may have had a prophetic quality. Clydebank historian Ian Johnston:

> When Clydebank won the order for the *QE2* I think it was like good old times again. But in fact the construction of the ship was shrouded with a degree of difficulty. And I think John Brown and Company actually lost money building the ship, I don't think there's any secret in that. Okay, they'd won another Cunarder, but . . . there was a degree of despair about the whole thing, the way the ship was built.

For a time there was a place for liners like the *QE2*. And there was something comfortingly Cunard about *Queen Elizabeth 2*. John Maxtone-Graham recounts:

> I made the discovery that, boarding *QE2* when . . . you go

OPPOSITE:
The *France* had just over a decade of service on the Atlantic run before, in September 1974, the French Government cut her desperately needed subsidy and her sailings ended.

The *Queen Elizabeth 2* sails majestically under New York's Verrazano-Narrows Bridge as she completes her maiden voyage to New York in May 1969. People line the road along the Narrows in Brooklyn to welcome her.

through that telescopic gangway and enter the ship, by some extraordinary alchemy it smells exactly like *Queen Mary* and *Queen Elizabeth*. The whole range of products and finishes and surfaces . . . that went together to make *QE2* are quite different from the corkoid and panelling of the *Queen Mary* and the *Queen Elizabeth*, but the ship smells the same.

Claude Villers was conscious of ambience, too:
> On the *United States* . . . the ambience was really like the taxis of New York . . . it wasn't fantastic. The English, of course, there was a delicious antiquated style on board their liners . . . and at

eleven o'clock they brought you an infusion and the little biscuits, and so that was very 'British' . . .

British or not, Cunard had sentenced the old *Queen*s to death even before the *QE2* had her maiden voyage. Both were sold, the *Queen Mary* for $3,400,000, and the *Queen Elizabeth* for double that, at $7,750,000. The older liner is now a floating hotel and museum off Long Beach, California. The *Queen Elizabeth* caught fire in Hong Kong harbour, during an expensive refit as an educational cruise-ship, in 1972. Like *Normandie*, she capsized under the weight of water poured

into her, and after a couple of years as a tourist spectacle, and a brief appearance in one of the James Bond films, she was ignominiously scrapped.[1]

The new *Queen*'s only 'superliner' companions were the speedy *United States* and the gastronomically renowned *France*. But by 1974, twelve years after her gala introduction, the *France* had fallen on hard times. Jean-Paul Herbert, archivist of the French Line collection at Le Havre:

> She had done very well for her five years, but things began to deteriorate by 1967. A year later, there were student riots all over France. There was also great labour unrest. Expenses, wages,

the cost of fuel increased in an immeasurable way. The *France* had started to decline and to become more and more expensive to operate. Her defeat came in 1974 when the French government agreed to end the subsidy to the ship. That was the end of the dream. Both the French Line and the government had done everything to make the ship more profitable and more popular. They added more and more cruises and introduced two trips around the world. But it was too late. The annual subsidy would have had to be increased from $14 million annually to $24 million. The monies went instead to the new *Concorde* project.

Hong Kong: the *Queen Elizabeth*, for years the world's largest passenger liner, rolls over on to her side after being consumed by flames, and sinks slowly in 120 feet of water in the city's harbour on 10 January 1972.

129

The supersonic airliner would be a symbol of the *entente cordiale* rather than of national pride, since it was a joint product with the British but, like the *France*, it was not an economical proposition.

In September 1974, some crew members on the *France* mutinied off Le Havre, holding the giant liner at anchor in the English Channel while demanding that she be restored and that they receive a 35 percent wage increase. It was now a hopeless situation for the future of the ship. Soon the *France* was sent to a Le Havre backwater to await disposal. For five years she swayed at anchor, rusting visibly, until she was bought for conversion to a cruise-ship by the Norwegian shipping magnate Knut Kloster.

Claude Villers saw *France* leave le Havre:

> There were thousands of people, and we saw the boat leave, pulled along by its tugboat, while all the other liners who had come had their flags at half-mast as if in mourning, and there were these heart-rending sounds of sirens, and it really seemed like when you slaughter a pig. It cries. We had killed the French merchant marine, because then it was finished, there were no more French liners.

On the North Atlantic, the end was nigh. Hapag-Lloyd (a combination of the old Hamburg-Amerika Line and the North German Lloyd) and Canadian Pacific withdrew in 1971, Holland America made its final Atlantic crossing two years later and within three years the Italian Line vanished as well. The initial hopes that the *Michelangelo* and *Raffaello* might enjoy long and profitable lives were far from correct. By 1970, both were losing money at an embarrassing rate for their government sponsors. On some occasions, the crew members outnumbered the fare-paying guests. In 1977, *Michelangelo* and *Raffaello* were part of a deal with the Shah of Iran's government. Their days ended in eastern waters: the *Raffaello* was sunk in an Iraqi air raid in 1983; the *Michelangelo* was sold to Pakistani scrappers in 1991.

Twenty years on, at the time of writing in early 1997, there are only two passenger-ship services remaining to remind the world of the former 'ocean greyhounds'. Cunard's *QE2* still spends about half her year on the Southampton–New York run, making six-day passages from one port to another. (In 1986–87, Cunard invested over $160 million in her, more than twice her original construction cost some twenty years before.) The only other service is run by the St Helena Shipping Company's 6,700-ton, 128-passenger *St Helena*. She sails regularly from Cardiff to serve the remote islands of St Helena, Napoleon's place of exile in the lonely South Atlantic.

BACK TO THE FUTURE

Long before the airliner was even thought of, scheduled cruises to remote and exotic places had been introduced by shipping lines as an off-season use for their liners. The salt-air environment was considered by physicians as therapeutic for many ailments, particularly those related to respiratory problems. 'Take a long sea voyage' was the advice often given to patients, and for those who could afford the fare, the experience usually resulted in a general improvement. Whether the salt air had anything to do with the improvement in a passenger's health or not, there was a market for cruises, and a new area of potential profit for the shipping companies to exploit.

P&O was the first company to capitalize on this alternative use of their ships. In 1844, William Thackeray, a young English author who would later rise to great literary heights, was given free passage on one of the company's early cruises of the Mediterranean. In return, he wrote a book on his experiences which greatly helped the company to popularize cruising. 'The Peninsular and Oriental Company had arranged an excursion in the Mediterranean by which,' wrote Thackeray, 'in the space of a couple of months, as many men and cities were to be seen as Ulysses surveyed and noted in ten years.' He went on to encourage 'all persons who have time and means to make a similar journey'.[2] P&O's investment in a free ticket certainly paid off as the young author eulogized the company and the cruising experience at great length in his writings.

When it came to an endorsement of the health benefits of cruising, the same company could not have believed their luck on reading an article in the *British Medical Journal*,

OPPOSITE:

An early Orient Line cruise poster from 1898. Orient were the first to use liners for cruising in the 1880s to destinations as far as the Norwegian fjords, and the Caribbean.

published in the 1880s, which began, 'The announcement by the Peninsular and Oriental Navigation Company of a new and low scale of charges for accommodation on board their magnificent ships has a special interest for medical men and their patients.' After a long explanation of the advantages to be derived from a sea voyage with excursions ashore, it winds up with a glowing mention of the company and the fares charged, and recognition of 'the importance of the step which the Company has taken in popularising ocean travel'. As early as 1904 the word 'cruises' was regularly used to promote this form of voyage by P&O.

The popularity of those early 'cruises' soon encouraged other lines to consider offering similar services, particularly in the northern hemisphere off-season when conditions on the North Atlantic discouraged travel by all who could possibly avoid such an experience. The warmer Mediterranean and, later, the Bahamas and the West Indies in the Caribbean became much more pleasant alternatives for both ships and passengers than the bitter cold winds, mountainous seas, and the dreaded ice floes of the stormy winter Atlantic.

The major differences between a 'cruise' and regular, scheduled passenger service are worth defining. With cruising, there is no necessity for sustained high speed in all weathers. Lower speeds in adverse conditions are far more conducive to passenger comfort and also require far less fuel. A scheduled service operates between major ports transporting passengers from A to B, whereas a cruise almost invariably completes a circuit of ports, returning passengers to the port of embarkation. On regular passenger services, the ships catered for a clearly defined class structure, where money dictated space and comfort. As cruising developed, one-class ships evolved. In many ways they are two very different operations requiring different services and facilities. Traditional passenger liners were less concerned with the creature comforts they provided. Arriving and departing on time and on schedule was the prime concern of the owners and the designers of ships built for this very specific purpose. Cruising, on the other hand, is all about passenger comfort and enjoyment, with itineraries carefully designed to create an environment of timelessness.

The transition between vessels designed as 'ocean greyhounds' and today's-palatial cruise liners which are themselves a highly marketed 'destination' – providing everything that a passenger wants in terms of a holiday – has been a slow, evolving process that began almost as soon as the first liners began operating regular services on the sea

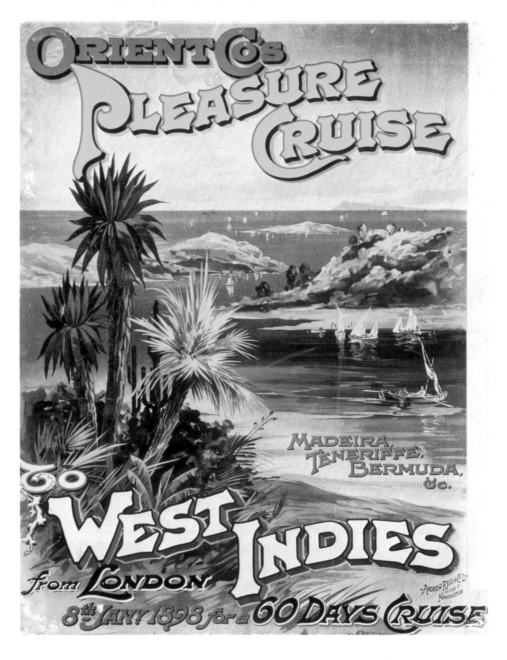

lanes of the world. So although the introduction of the jet airliner brought about sweeping and quite radical changes in ships and the services they offered, all based largely on survival, cruising goes back to well before the turn of the century.

It is usually agreed that the Hamburg-Amerika Line built the world's first cruise-ship, the *Prinzessin Victoria Luise* of 1900. Although only 4,400 tons and 407ft (122m) in length, her small size was a deliberate decision: she was designed to resemble the royal yachts of Europe and therefore attract a very specific clientele. Her passengers were to be only the very rich. For the first time aboard any commercial passenger ship, each cabin had a complete bedroom, private sitting-room and full bathroom. Sadly, within six years, in 1906, she went aground on Jamaica during a Caribbean trip and became a complete wreck.

Hamburg-Amerika's interest in big-ticket cruising continued, however, though not yet to the extent of building cruise-only vessels. When the sister ships *Cleveland* and *Cincinnati* were built in 1909, they were quite novel in being designed not only for class-divided North Atlantic sailings, but also for luxury cruising during the slack season in winter. From January 1910, the *Cleveland* offered a wintertime circumnavigation of the globe, an extraordinary 100-day trip that was booked by 650 travellers. In a short time, the *Cincinnati* joined her sister ship in these lavish sailings.

Hamburg-Amerika also converted unsuccessful liners for the cruising market. The 16,700-ton *Deutschland* had won the Blue Riband but paid for her speed with unacceptable noise and vibration. In 1910 she was returned to the shipyard for conversion. She was repainted all-white (still traditional for summer cruising) and her original 2,050 berths in four classes became 487, all first class. She was even renamed the *Victoria Luise*, a deliberate link to the highly acclaimed *Prinzessin Victoria Luise*. Equipped with a grill room, a full gymnasium and even a canvas swimming pool on deck, she roamed the West Indies, the Mediterranean and the Norwegian coast.

After the First World War, even the world's largest and most celebrated liners, such as Cunard's speedy *Mauretania* and the splendid 46,000-ton *Aquitania*, sought employment away from the ferocious North Atlantic in winter. Temporarily made over into an all first-class ship, the *Mauretania* might travel for six or eight weeks to the French Riviera – 200 or so millionaires being looked after by 800 staff.

By the late Twenties and into the early Thirties, world cruising became an established social ritual for the wealthy. The *Franconia* usually sailed from New York just after the Christmas–New Year holidays – often starting at midnight – and then returned in late May or early June. In a 1931 advertisement, the ship's next world cruise was publicized:

> Faraway glamorous places have stirred your imagination! Bali, still in its primitive civilization; Macassar, flaming like a ruby on the jungle's edge; Bangkok's regal splendour; and Saigon, remote and so special. The *Franconia* includes them without extra cost . . . and such unique spots as Athens and the Holy Land . . . and all the other highlights of a Round-the-World voyage. 140 days, 33 ports of call and all at greatly reduced rates, beginning at $750.

Perhaps no world cruise in the 1930s, however, quite equalled those of Canadian Pacific's giant *Empress of Britain*, a 42,000-ton dreamboat so well appointed that she even featured a tennis court on her top deck. For these voyages, her capacity was especially reduced to 750 from 1,195 to create a more club-like atmosphere.

In the foreshadowing of later events in the world of cruising, a Norwegian line, the Bergen Line, took a new step in cruising. It commissioned a ship that was deliberately and clearly styled after sumptuous private yachts. She was the *Stella Polaris* (the 'star of the north'). The 5,200-ton ship carried some 165 staff for an equal number of guests. Her interiors were fitted in polished woods and a small swimming pool was placed aft. Handsomely raked, her profile appeared beautiful and serene. Boarding at Malta in 1930, English novelist Evelyn Waugh wrote for *Harper's Bazaar*, 'The *Stella* came from Norway and brought a cold buffet of Baltic delicacies, which is the best I have ever encountered.'

Even in the Depression era of the 1930s, short ocean voyages became escapes for many, even if only temporarily.

There were short runs to Bermuda, Nassau and Havana from New York, and even summertime northern passages to Halifax, Nova Scotia. Cheapest of all were the overnight 'cruises to nowhere', parties at sea with all bars open despite the rigours of prohibition. From these so-called 'booze cruises', thousands began to graduate to slightly longer sailings: 4 days to Bermuda, 6 days to Nassau, 8 to Havana.

John Maxtone-Graham recalls such voyages in the 1930s: During the Depression the *Berengaria* would come into New York from Southampton, rigidly separated into classes. She'd tie up at Pier 54, passengers would get off and then a new breed of passenger would come on for a three or four-day cruise to Bermuda. And all these passengers were one class . . . and what happened was that the first-class public rooms which were designed to hold 600–700 people suddenly had to hold 1200.

By the end of the 1930s there was a wide variety of cruises available to passengers ranging from the super-wealthy to the financially comfortable. European and American lines mounted cruises of all kinds from the great ports of New York, San Francisco, Southampton and Cherbourg to eternally popular destinations: the Mediterranean, the Caribbean, the Pacific islands or (in summer only) the Norwegian fiords. Only the outbreak of war in 1939 put a stop to the growth of cruising, but even that war did not last for ever, and the rich are always with us.

The first big liner built by Cunard specifically for full-time cruising was the *Caronia* of 1948. A 34,100-tonner that often carried as few as 350 passengers on her long-distance leisure travels (her actual cruise capacity was 600 and absolute maximum was 932), she had the overall feel of a floating country club. Nicknamed the 'Green Goddess' because of her unique colouring, the *Caronia* went around the world almost every winter (otherwise, she did a grand tour of the entire Pacific) and then cruised the Mediterranean and Scandinavia. John Maxtone-Graham recalls: 'She was so select that you couldn't buy segments [of the world cruise]. On *Caronia* you bought the whole trip or not at all. Some Americans used to empty their cabin and let their children use it, but they had paid for the entire circumnavigation of the globe.'

Deck games in 1935.

There were tales of passengers, women especially, who lived on board for months and sometimes years at a time. One elderly lady, Miss Clara MacBeth, still holds the all-time record of fourteen years! One passenger chartered an entire railway coach during a shore excursion in India, another gave a party for 300 fellow passengers at Hong Kong's Repulse Bay Hotel and still others regularly flew in personal physicians and nurses. A couple of *Caronia* passengers recall:

Sailing day was like a big, happy reunion. There were so many repeaters and everyone knew one another from years and years of travelling together. Once under way, these passengers threw great theme parties – 'Emerald Night' and 'Chinese Night' and 'Arabian Nights' – and invited hundreds of fellow passengers. They paid for all the drinks, but the ship provided the other refreshments, including 'towers of fresh shrimp'. Being invited to one of these parties made for wonderful memories.

By the 1960s, the most popular cruise-ship in Britain was Royal Mail Lines' *Andes*, a 25,500-tonner that dated from

1939 and was converted for cruising in 1959–60. Her two- and three-week-long sailings were immensely popular and often booked a year or more in advance. John Draffin served in the purser's department on the *Andes* and remembers:

> She was an exceptionally elegant ship, much like a floating country club. Sailing day from Southampton was like the first day back at school. Almost all the passengers were 'regulars' and therefore knew one another. The 'Who's Who' of Britain would be on board. Passengers in the best suites brought along their own servants. There were, of course, more crew members than needed, but then that was the Royal Mail Lines' standard. There were special considerations and facilities for older passengers. While we always carried a full dance band, the demand was, in fact, for very limited entertainment. It was a very quiet, elegant lifestyle on board. The *Andes* catered to aristocratic Britain.

Before long, things would be rather different in the highly specialized world of the modern cruise liner.

GLOBALIZATION: THE SHIP AS THE DESTINATION

In 1979 Margaret Thatcher became Prime Minister of Britain. It was an event that signalled, among other things, a change in economic and social structures not only in Britain but across the world. The foreign policies of Mrs Thatcher and President Reagan would lead to the collapse of Communism in Europe. Domestic policies, such as financial deregulation, privatization and sweeping income-tax reductions, would enable a greater proportion of the populations of Europe and the United States to increase consumption of goods and services (though a smaller proportion found themselves without homes, jobs or welfare). Now, cruising holidays, among many other things, would no longer be available only to the seriously rich.

By coincidence, also in 1979, there was an event of real as well as symbolic significance for the world of great ships. The last of the great French liners, the *France*, was towed from the anchorage where she had been rusting since 1974 to be converted to a cruise-ship for the Norwegian shipowner Knut Kloster. She was renamed *Norway*. In June 1980 she

steamed into Miami, the largest ship in what had already become the billion-dollar Caribbean cruising industry. Before long, far bigger ships, the successors of the old 'ocean greyhounds' would be built, and the billions would multiply.

The story really begins fifteen years earlier, in the mid-1960s, when history had already begun to repeat itself. Just as in the mid-nineteenth century, when Cunard, Collins and later competitors such as Ballin and Ismay, had fought for control of the lucrative passenger trade on the North Atlantic, now there was a struggle for a new kind of cruise trade that promised to become ever more profitable. It would be based, not on the old liner ports like New York, but on the Florida holiday town of Miami.

If a date had to be chosen as the start of the boom in the Florida cruise business it would be 19 December 1966, when a new, purpose-built cruise-ship, the *Sunward*, entered service in Florida. It was operated by Norwegian Caribbean Lines, which was in fact a legal fiction dreamed up by the two partners in the venture, the Norwegian Knut Kloster and the Israeli Ted Arison. Kloster had the ship, Arison the ideas, and the name of the company would sum up the cruise business in Miami.[3] Perhaps because of their cool summers and bleak winters, Scandinavians and especially Norwegians had enjoyed a long tradition of cruises in the sunshine. Also, Norway had a large shipbuilding industry and, like Greece, a smattering of big shipowners. Whatever the reason, Norwegians would have an impressive part in building the Caribbean industry, as would often be reflected in the names of the new cruise lines yet to be launched. There would be new ships, too, no longer built on the Clyde or in Belfast but in a different tradition. Professor Slaven says: 'There were designs for new generations of very tall ships with huge recreational and restaurant space. And . . . the Finnish and Baltic ferry designs were in a sense the beginnings of the new generation of cruise-ship designs.'

Edward Stephan, Vice-Chairman of Royal Caribbean Cruise Lines remembers the transformation of the industry as he saw it:

> I had been running a company called Commodore Cruise Lines. And we were bringing out another vessel, a converted car ferry.

We . . . brought it up to the latest safety standards, filled in the empty space with passenger cabins and public space, and that ship became the *Boheme* for Commodore Cruise Lines. Already I'd gone to Norway to try and interest Norwegian owners in building new ships . . . At that time I was looking out mostly for safety, and we needed a maritime nation that really knew what they were doing. Could have been any of the Scandinavian countries.

Edward Stephan initiated many of the features that became standard on the big Miami cruise-ships, like cocktail lounges with a view:

I think it was probably ignorance is bliss. We saw the Space Needle at the World's Fair in Seattle. We said, okay, for these new ships we're building, *Song of Norway* and so on, we want to get rid of the smoke-stack. The smoke-stack's always ugly. So here we said let's have a lounge right up there where the people can look out. And everybody said that's crazy. One, it'd vibrate like crazy . . . and two, it just isn't done. Finally, we found some young Finnish architects who worked and worked and finally came up with it. And we put in a newspaper ad . . . this Viking Crown (lounge) and a couple of seagulls going over the top. And we sold the ship out that way.

Cocktails at sunset, high above the decks, in a bar incorporated in the funnel – a sensational innovation introduced in the early 1970s on Royal Caribbean Line's super luxury sister ships *Sun Viking, Song of Norway* and *Nordic Prince.*

The line targeted California as its main market, and soon established air-sea packages operating with 747 services out of San Francisco and Los Angeles. Royal Caribbean Cruise Lines began to make money by the bucketful.

Like bees to nectar, other cruise lines followed RCCL to Miami. The Norwegian Bergen Line, which had, before the Second World War, launched the ultra-luxurious cruise-ship *Stella Polaris*, headed a new consortium under the name of Royal Viking Line. They targeted the upper end of the market as they had before, and encouraged repeat sailings by an early form of loyalty reward along the lines of the later 'Frequent Flyer' schemes. By 1973 they had three new vessels sailing from Miami: *Royal Viking Star, Royal Viking Sun* and *Royal Viking Sea*.

In 1974 the venerable P&O took over the financially ailing Princess Lines to add to their existing cruise fleet, and were soon re-equipping it with new vessels. Over the next few years new lines were formed and reformed, chief executives came and went, and the Caribbean cruising industry continued to grow. From a scruffy little port, best known for drug-running, Miami became the world headquarters for cruising. And nothing put cruising on the map as effectively as a piece of serendipitous fantasy.

It was in 1977 that television producer Aaron Spelling approached Princess Lines to see if they would help with a TV series he had planned, by allowing filming on their cruise-ships. The series was *The Love Boat*, and Princess Lines was astute enough to realize that the publicity from the series could bring in a lot of customers, if Spelling got it right. Both Spelling and Princess were successful to an extent far beyond their wildest dreams. *The Love Boat* caught on all over the world, appealing to the romantic dreams of the mass market, who saw in the screen fantasy the sort of world they wanted to inhabit. It was an attainable fantasy, and it was the keynote of what the cruise market was selling, as they soon realized. After *The Love Boat* everyone knew just what the market was demanding, and set out to supply it in whatever way they could.

If there is one shipping line that epitomizes the thrills and spills and ultimate success of the last twenty-odd years, it is Carnival Lines. Its founder, Israeli-born Ted Arison, had set up the pioneering Norwegian Caribbean Cruise Line with Oslo shipping magnate, Knut Kloster. But in 1971, after a disagreement with Kloster, Arison decided to set up on his own. After collecting a million US dollars for his side of the partnership, he started to put together the elements of a new cruise line. Meshulam Riklis, an old friend from Israel, had a successful travel business in Boston, and was using the name 'Carnival' for tours. Together, Arison and Riklis set up Carnival Cruise Lines, and bought the old *Empress of Canada*. To maintain the carnival theme, they renamed her *Mardi Gras* and set about earning money from her.

Bob Dickinson, now President of Carnival Cruise Lines – the largest and most successful cruise line in the world – lived through most of the story. The *Mardi Gras* was advertised as 'The Flagship of the Golden Fleet', but, as Dickinson says, 'It wasn't golden and there was no fleet, and it was just a disaster.' There was no time to convert the ship before she sailed on her first cruise, 'so we had 200 carpenters and plumbers on board, clanging and banging away on the vessel while people were trying to enjoy their cruise. So the first year and a half or so we lost $8 million.' Then, 'we realized we were in the vacation business, not the cruise business, and people came on board to have a vacation. So we thought of the ship as the destination . . . And we coined the name 'Fun Ship' and brought that into the marketing. And we cut the loss in half in 1974 and turned a profit in 1975, and never looked back.'

John Maxtone-Graham has followed the Carnival story from the beginning:

> The thing about Carnival that you sense when you get on board their ships, and I've sailed with them only once, and apart from the slightly gaudy look of things and the noise level and the mass passengers they attract, the thing that is almost palpable is their success. And the ships reek of success. And they have now, I think, 30 percent or 35 percent of the market, and that's a big chunk of business. And the other thing about Carnival Cruise Line's upper echelon, all their top people, they don't change at all. They have honed a very good team and they make it work.

Joseph Farcas is the architect of the Carnival ships. He has a

design philosophy that realizes the ideas behind Bob Dickinson's 'Fun Ship' concept:

> I call it entertainment architecture. And it leads me to my favourite analogy, my explanation of what I'm trying to do for the guests on Carnival Cruise Lines. Movies. I think everyone enjoys the movies . . . Well, what do you do when you watch a movie? You pay your money, you go into the theatre, you sit down in your chair, the lights go down, it becomes a dark room and the screen lights up and you see these images on the screen and this fantasy action, whatever it is. My belief is that most people sitting in their solitude in the darkness are saying to themselves 'I wish that I were on that screen.' And that's what I'm trying to do. I'm trying to take people out of their normal everyday lives and put them into a glamorous world that most people are just not enjoying on an everyday basis. And that is the *raison d'être* for what I do on the ships.

Bill Drier's advertising agency has worked with Carnival since 1984. He has seen their success. 'Carnival is sailing at over 100 percent occupancy. And the way they get there is they figure two persons per room, and if there are more than that in a room, say a room that has extra beds, that counts as over 100 percent. So they're a very successful cruise line.' It wasn't always so, as Bob Dickinson explains:

> We were the runt of the litter of the cruise industry. We were on the lowest rung of the food chain of cruising. The passengers then, the average age, we say kiddingly, was deceased. Cruising was for old people and their parents . . . So we purposely marketed to people under the age of death to get families with young children . . . on board cruise-ships. The thinking being that if we could get somebody to try cruising in their teens, twenties or thirties, they'd have many more years of opportunity to repeat the cruise, rather than to market to somebody in their twilight years when they wouldn't have that many more opportunities to come cruise with us.

The oil crisis of the mid-Seventies came and went, with some casualties, but Ted Arison and his line survived and prospered. In due course, Carnival would not only have the world's largest cruise fleet, but would convince more

OPPOSITE:
Of all newcomers to the cruise-ship industry, Royal Viking Line was the most deluxe and select for the 1970s. Ships such as their *Royal Viking Star* made voyages from 3 days to 100 days and on itineraries that covered the globe.

RIGHT:
Concentrating on the Caribbean and with summertime voyages to Alaska, Princess Cruises today offers voyages to every corner of the globe.

OPPOSITE:
The 1,500 seat Palladium Theatre on Carnival Line's *Destiny* is reputed to be the most sophisticated cruise-ship theatre ever created, with every stage technique used in the world's leading productions available. Five decks deep, this theatre is a revolution in on-board entertainment facilities.

travellers to take their first cruise than any other company. Arison had bought two more second-hand liners by 1978, and then built his first brand-new ship, the 36,000-ton *Tropicale*, two years later.

In the late 1970s, after Carnival had shown the way, it seemed obvious that the other mass-market cruise lines needed ever-larger ships to compete with Carnival. In 1978, Royal Caribbean Cruise Lines sent two of its original three cruise-ships, the *Song of Norway* and *Nordic Prince*, back to their Finnish builders. To meet increased demands, they had to be lengthened and their capacities increased. The 550ft (165m) ships were fitted with 85ft (25.5m) mid-sections. With added cabins, this increased their capacities from 724 to 1,040, in anticipation of the 'cruise boom' of the 1980s.

Amazingly, the entire process was completed on each ship within little more than three months. Similarly, the three Royal Viking Line sister ships were 'stretched', in the early 1980s, with 90-ft (27-m) insertions. Their capacities increased from 536 to 758. Edward Stephan explains the reasons behind the shift to bigger ships, 'Basically you sail with the same deck and engine crew whether you're a smaller ship or a larger ship, give or take a few. And you have all these economies of scale . . . particularly on the maintenance.' The enlargements even created partly unsuspected advantages:

> And the strange thing about it was the relative public space per passenger inside and outside was more than it was before. The extra 85ft (25.5m) . . . was all pure passenger space. We didn't need any more engines or anything. At the same time, we found out on our vessels we didn't use any more fuel because when you lengthen the ship, the water along the hull lines gives you a flow that in reality uses very little more fuel. So now the fuel per passenger goes down because you split it among 1,000 passengers instead of 700.

In 1979 Knut Kloster's Norwegian Caribbean Lines had pioneered the giant cruise-ship. Company managers and engineers looked at existing, but laid-up, tonnage to rehabilitate into a truly huge cruise-ship – perhaps the *United States, Michelangelo, Raffaello* or *France*. The last was to be the final choice. A deficit-ridden transatlantic liner, she had, by 1979, been moored at her Le Havre backwater for five years and her only destination seemed likely to be the scrapyard. Norwegian Caribbean Lines, Kloster's company, much to the complete surprise of the entire cruise industry, saw the 66,300-ton *France* quite differently. With an extensive remake, and lavish and loving cosmetic surgery, she could become the ideal cruise-ship. She would be transformed from indoor Atlantic liner to an outdoor tropical liner. There would be some economy measures: reducing the engine space, a cut in the size of her crew and an increase in her total passenger capacity. But more importantly, on board were introduced lavishly colourful lounges, bars and casinos, an outdoor restaurant and a theatre that presented full

Broadway and Las Vegas-style productions. Recommissioned as the *Norway* in May 1980 after a total investment of $130 million, she was the world's largest cruise liner. Kloster's company seemed to have made a pre-emptive strike on its competitors, but they would soon strike back.

When, later, huge cruise-ships were built from the ground up, traditional methods were turned on their head. The yards in Finland, Norway, Germany, France and Italy were no longer building 'ocean greyhounds', and they accordingly changed their work practices to suit the market. Carnival's designer, Joseph Farcas says:

Naval architecture . . . has advanced to the point where today, most ships are modular. So you have very few different cabin types. That allows the cabins to be built in either a prefabricated

The title of the world's largest cruise liner will be held by the 105,000-ton *Grand Princess* when she begins sailing in 1998. As part of P&O Princess Cruises' $3 billion expansion programme, *Grand Princess* will cater for 2,600 passengers. She will feature a virtual reality centre, a wedding and renewal of vows chapel, a glass-roofed night-club suspended over the stern of the ship, five swimming pools and an unprecedented 750 cabins with private balconies.

They promise to take fantasy further than ever. Dining, for example, will be a unique, even bizarre experience. As passengers arrive in the restaurant, the whimsically named Animator's Palate, the room is almost completely black and white. Then, as the meal is served, the entire room begins to change as colours begin to appear on the walls, the ceilings and even at the tables. Synchronized light and sound will accompany each change until, by the end of the meal, the restaurant is filled with the colours of an animated movie. In effect, the passengers will actually be part of the movie, part of a designer's fantasy, inhabiting an imaginary world. Even the exterior will satisfy the public's thirst for fantasy, as the ships are designed subtly to recall the classic liners of the 1930s, like the *Queen Mary* and *Queen Elizabeth*, while the interiors will carry more than a hint of the Art Deco that characterized *Ile de France* and *Normandie*. Of course, the Disney characters will feature in the decoration of the two vessels.

Knut Kloster, whose original venture with Ted Arison arguably started off the whole cruising boom, is dreaming now what many experts believe is an impossible dream. It is nothing less than a floating city. Originally known as the *Phoenix*, the 250,000-ton, 1,250ft (375m)-long *America World City* would cost over $1 billion. With a width of 100yd (91m), she would carry a 2,000-seat theatre, a 100,000-book library, a stock brokerage office, an art gallery, several pools and a complete American main street.

'The America World City Project is a programme to develop, design, build and operate a new class of passenger ship, the largest the world has ever seen,' says John S. Rogers, the chief spokesperson for the America World City Corporation in New York. He continues:

Some tankers have a larger hull, but aside from that, these will be the biggest ships afloat. They would be more than twice the size of the *Destiny* and the *Grand Princess*, and have three times the physical capacity. The ships would have three towers on top of a three-deck high 'downtown'. That 'downtown' will be like an aircraft carrier. The overall length is just under $1/4$ mile (0.4km). If you were to stand on the very top of the ship, you would be standing on the equivalent of the 21st floor of an office building on shore. These ships will be very big. But they will be able to sail under New York's Verrazano Bridge and San Francisco's Golden Gate. And getting into a port will never be an impediment because the ship will have its own auxiliary transportation system in the form of four, very large day cruisers with capacities of 400 each. The *America World City* will be able to use even the smaller harbour, bringing passengers to and from the mother ship. She will draw approximately 33ft (10m) of water. She is not in a race for size or actually setting any sort of record. Instead, she will be a new generation, a market-driven product, which is designed not as a cruise-ship. It goes past the evolution in the use of passenger ships to a new stage.

Rogers sees the project as also going past the concept of ship as destination, to the idea of 'ship as real estate'. For financial reasons an essential part of the project is that the vessel should be built in an US shipyard and registered under the American flag. Only in this way can she legally be used between US ports, where her passengers will originate, so that she can, for example, cruise down the east coast, picking up and dropping off cruise passengers from port to port, and entering even the smaller ports by using the 400-berth

PREVIOUS PAGE, TOP:
The Walt Disney Company enters the cruise line business. Disney's first ship, the 85,000-ton *Disney Magic* will set sail out of Port Canaveral, Florida, in March 1998. A sister ship, *Disney Wonder*, will enter service nine months later, in December 1998.

PREVIOUS PAGE, BOTTOM LEFT:
The main lobby on *Disney Magic*: Art Deco inspired, and reminiscent of classic liners of the past, it will also include a blend of well-known Disney characters as part of the decor.

PREVIOUS PAGE, BOTTOM RIGHT:
America World City Corporation's 250,000-ton *America World City* by the American artist Robert T. McCall. This painting is currently displayed at Port Canaveral, Florida, which has been nominated as home port for the proposed *America World City*. The ship, a virtual floating city, will be managed and marketed by Westin Hotels & Resorts.

tenders. Although no US shipyard has built a large passenger vessel since the *United States* decades back, Rogers foresees subcontracting the construction so that the accommodation would be built by firms specializing in hotel construction rather than by shipbuilders. Rogers suggests that the ship, or city, would be many things: hotel, casino, convention centre as well as cruiser. He imagines a future in which the *America World City* will, for instance, visit Sydney for the Olympic Games, representing, at one stroke, a 25 percent increase in hotel accommodation.

It is fair to say that not many experts believe that *America World City* will ever sail. John Maxtone-Graham says: 'I'm afraid the moment has passed. I still get enquiries about it, but I don't think it's going to sail any more than the *United States* is going to sail again. I mean, these are lost causes that I'm afraid the moment has passed by.' On the other hand, experts might not have imagined that *France* would become *Norway*, or that, in a sense, Miami would become New York. The future is full of surprises, and while Kloster's dream may seem unattainable, much the same might have been said a century and a half ago of the dreams of men like Samuel Cunard or Isambard Brunel. The great liners of the past were not only transport, but the embodiment of romance and fantasy. If a ship can be a destination, and a cruise can be a movie, a floating city may not be too wild a dream.

THE EMPIRE STRIKES BACK: THE BIG WHITE WHALE

Back in 1982, after Knut Kloster had waved his magic wand and turned *France* into *Norway*, and when the Florida wharves were already echoing with the tramp of an army of tourists, grim reality burst upon the scene in the cold South Atlantic, by coincidence not far from where Brunel's *Great Britain* had been beached before her belated rescue.

Argentina had for many years been urging Britain to give up the colony that Argentina calls the Islas Malvinas, and Britain calls the Falkland Islands. Because Argentina was relatively close geographically to the islands, most trade and communication came through that country, and visitors from Argentina were not uncommon. But in April 1982 a number

of unwelcome visitors, in the shape of an Argentine invasion force, arrived on the beaches around the capital of the islands, Port Stanley. Within a few hours they had overwhelmed the few British marines who defended the islands and raised the blue and white flag of Argentina.

The government in London was surprised and aghast that, after years of diplomacy, the Argentine government had lost patience and resorted to armed force. The Prime Minister, Margaret Thatcher, was not inclined to let them get away with one of the last remaining vestiges of the British Empire, however cold and barren it might appear to be. Both Mrs Thatcher and the Argentine dictator, General Galtieri, had domestic political problems which could be reduced by appeals to patriotism and national feeling, and a little sabre-rattling. Within a few weeks the Argentine troops on the Falklands woke up to find that a British Royal Naval task force and several thousand men were upon them and that a full-scale war was about to happen.

The Falklands lie in cold, often iceberg-infested seas not very far from the South Pole. The nearest continent is South America, and the nearest coast that of Argentina. Apart from the one runway at Port Stanley, which was now held by the Argentine troops, there was no friendly airstrip for transport aircraft for thousands of miles. Any substantial British fighting force would have to arrive by sea. It was a situation the British military high command had faced since the earliest days of the Empire. To overcome the giant logistical problem of defending their colonial interests scattered around the globe, the fleets of passenger liners owned and operated by British companies had always, without fail, answered the call to duty.

Even as far back as the Crimean War in 1854, eleven Cunarders, eleven P&O steamers and the *Great Britain* had been requisitioned to serve as troop-ships and hospital-ships. Regular British steamship services were interrupted or cancelled altogether, while the nation's shipping lines did their patriotic duty, and one result of the participation in the war was that the British Royal Navy at last decided to adopt steam for their warships. In 1982, just as in the conflicts of 1854, 1914 and 1939, Britain turned to its merchant marine for supply-ships,

LEFT:
P&O's 1952 *Uganda* joined the British India Steam Navigation Company as a passenger/cargo liner on the UK/East Africa service before being converted, in 1967, for educational cruising. On 10 April 1982 she was requisitioned for the Falklands War and converted for use as a hospital-ship.

BELOW:
HRH Prince of Wales and Captain Scott-Masson on board *Canberra* on her arrival back from the Falklands.

hospital-ships and troop-ships. But in those earlier years the ports of the world had been full of ships of all sizes, from coasters to great ocean liners, flying the British flag; now, the merchant fleet was greatly reduced. There were few great liners available that could carry thousands of troops safely through the stormy Atlantic to the Falklands. But there were two, belonging to the two great steamship companies, Cunard and P&O. They were the *QE2* and the *Canberra*.

Admiral of the Fleet, Lord Lewin, the British Chief of Defence Staff at the time of the Falklands conflict, attended every meeting of the War Cabinet. He recalls: 'We were lucky the *Canberra* was in Southampton.' He went on to add:

We decided about halfway through that we had better send another brigade down. That's five thousand men. We looked around for ships to take them, and of course the *QE2* could take the lot, and it just so happened that she was due in from a cruise to Southampton the following Tuesday. This was about Thursday or Friday, and so I went to the War Cabinet and said that we needed the *QE2* to take this brigade out, and they all burst out laughing and said 'You can't be serious' . . . And John Nott, who

'The Great White Whale': P&O's *Canberra* returning to Southampton on 11 July 1982. She was given an unprecedented reception by the people of this historic port city.

was the Secretary of Defence said, 'Oh, I can't believe this, I'll go round to the Department of Trade and sort it out.' He came back two hours later and said, 'The Chief of Defence Staff is right, she's the only ship available.' And that's how the *QE2* got picked.

The captain of *Canberra* in 1982 was Dennis Scott-Masson.

We were in Naples when Galtieri invaded the Falkland Islands. Twenty-four hours later, when we were between Naples and Gibraltar, we got a signal to say we were to call in at Gibraltar, and that it was possible the ship would be requisitioned by the government to carry troops. So we went into Gibraltar for a few minutes, picked up an advance party of Royal Marines and naval people and then proceeded back to Southampton, where we

146

were, in a remarkably short time, converted into – more than a troop-carrier – it was a troop-carrier, an assault-ship, hospital-ship. Three helicopter decks were put on board. Originally the idea was that we wouldn't actually go down into the Falklands, we'd only go down to the Total Exclusion Zone, about 200 miles (300km) off the Falklands, where we would transfer our troops to military transports. But, of course, that was very rapidly changed, and it was decided that there was only one way to get the troops in, and that was to land them from the *Canberra*.

The P&O liner was to carry a civilian crew, though they would be outnumbered by military personnel. 'We had a crew of 800-odd, and on the way back from Gibraltar to Southampton I asked how many would be prepared to go down south to the Falklands, and 100 percent volunteered. We only took 413, but they all volunteered, and in fact we took some of the women with us.'

The Cunard Line's flagship followed hard upon *Canberra*'s heels. Admiral Lord Lewin continues: 'the *QE2* was made available very quickly, but she couldn't really be exposed to danger. The thought of risking losing the ship that had the same name as the Sovereign was more than the politicians could bear. The fact that the *Canberra* was exposed didn't really matter.' Lord Lewin adds, with a whimsical smile, 'After all, it was only the capital of Australia. And so the *QE2* was sent to South Georgia, which is about 1,500 miles (2,250km) from Argentina and the *Canberra* . . . was sent over to South Georgia to transfer the men from the *QE2* and bring them across to the Falklands. So the *QE2* had an easy run down at 26 knots and back at 26 knots, and was never exposed to danger.'

Just like her great predecessors, *QE2* was converted from her usual trade to carry two or three times as many troops as she usually carried passengers. Peter Jackson was master of the *QE2* in the Falklands conflict of 1982: 'I was on leave at the time. And my wife came out to me in my little workshop in the garden to say that it had just been announced on the radio that the *Queen Elizabeth II* was going to be taken out of her transatlantic service and would be transformed into a troop-ship to take reinforcements down to the South

Atlantic.' Speed was essential:

When she came into Southampton, a plan had already been evolved with the ship repair yards, Vosper Thorneycroft's, and they went to work in virtually making the ship into a troop-ship, and it was all achieved in eight days, which was a most remarkable thing to do. They had to protect all the wonderful carpets and coverings on the bulkheads, and this was done with hardboard. And also they had to put on board helicopter landing pads. We were obviously going to be using helicopters quite a bit, and so three helicopter pads were constructed, almost like a jigsaw puzzle, and brought piecemeal on to the ship and welded in position. But in order to do that, they had virtually to destroy two lounges and they destroyed two swimming pools.

Unlike the *Queen Mary*, which had to carry some 15,000 men quite routinely during the Second World War, the *QE2* was only expected to carry about 4,000. Peter Jackson recalls:

The Gurkhas all arrived in buses and it was a remarkable picture to see them boarding the ship with all their equipment, and then the Scots Guards and the Welsh Guards all arrived, and they were allotted the various cabins that they were going to live in. And it was just a matter, really, of doubling up on the accommodation. The lounges were used as mess halls and things like that. The Gurkhas brought all their own cooks because they ate different foods to the Welsh Guards and the Scots Guards. And so it all worked out extremely well.

War is an untidy business and infrequently turns out as planners have predicted. The Falklands campaign was no exception, and the final assault was the result of many decisions made and countermanded. On 13 May, with the task force anchored off Ascension Island, it had been decided that the major assault would be on the port of San Carlos, about 40 miles (60km) from the capital, Port Stanley, and thought only to be lightly held by the Argentine forces. On 15 May, military discipline was imposed on all civilians on board *Canberra* in preparation for the coming landings. That afternoon, *Canberra* tested her machine-guns, and on the next day, a Sunday, Dennis Scott-Masson predicted 'an interesting and intriguing week' in his weekly message to the ship's company.[4] On Thursday, 20 May, *Canberra*'s chefs offered steak for breakfast, lunch and dinner.[5] It was the clearest of indications that the next day would be 'D-Day'. Dennis Scott-Masson goes on to say:

> There was only one night we didn't have wine with dinner, and that was the night we went into San Carlos. We approached the Falkland Sound between East and West Falkland late on the night of the 20th. We initially anchored in Falkland Sound about, I think it was, three o'clock in the morning, and then went into San Carlos Bay before daylight, and anchored in San Carlos Bay with the intent of being in a virtually landlocked harbour, so that it was difficult for the enemy aircraft to get a run at any of the ships.

The British had underestimated their enemy. After the Second World War the Argentine Air Force had had been trained by ex-*Luftwaffe* pilots, and this high standard of instruction continued to be upheld. The head of the Argentine Air Force, Brigadier General Lami Dozo, had proclaimed, 'We will die before we are dishonoured'. They were also equipped with the highly efficient and deadly French-made Exocet missiles.

While the task force had hoped for cloudy conditions to conceal their operations at San Carlos, the day of 21 May was clear and sunny. *Canberra* was anchored near the shore. After breakfast, the P&O officers admiring the view witnessed the awesome spectacle of the Argentine Pucara warplanes that suddenly breasted the hill and came in for the attack. *Canberra* became known with affection by the British fighting force as 'the great white whale' after Moby Dick in Herman Melville's novel, and her huge bulk glowed in the sunshine as wave after wave of aircraft 'hedgehopped' in for the kill.

'Our major fear,' recalls Scott-Masson, 'was that we would be hit by bombs or an Exocet missile . . . Of course the ship's superstructure was built of aluminium, and fire would have been our worst hazard, and that was what we worried about.' One of the British warships that had already been annihilated, the destroyer HMS *Sheffield*, had been hit by a low-flying Exocet missile and her aluminium structure had blazed fiercely.

Twenty minutes after the first attack by the Pucaras, more powerful Skyhawk and Mirage planes appeared over the waters of San Carlos Bay. Nearby, the frigates HMS *Yarmouth* and HMS *Plymouth* and the cruiser HMS *Antrim* cruised with their armaments ready to protect *Canberra*, and further out was a line of frigates: HMS *Ardent*, HMS *Broadsword*, HMS *Brilliant*, HMS *Argonaut* and HMS *Alacrity*. Against them that day were seventy-two aircraft flown with daring and brilliance by their Argentine pilots.

There were some close calls. 'There is footage of an explosion just astern of the ship,' said Scott-Masson, 'which could have been a missile coming towards the ship, which was blown out of the sky by one of the naval escorts that were looking after us. We were very, very lucky. We weren't scathed, nothing hit us, I've never understood quite why. We must have been a socking great target, the largest unit in San Carlos Bay, still painted white with gleaming yellow funnels, so we were pretty obvious. But, there we are, we got away with it.' The Royal Navy didn't. At the end of that day HMS *Ardent* had been sunk, HMS *Argonaut* badly damaged, and HMS *Antrim*, HMS *Brilliant* and HMS *Broadsword* had all been hit by bombs that fortunately failed to explode. *Canberra*'s escape was a miracle. 'Don't ask me why the Argentine Air Force failed to hit the *Canberra* in the Falkland Sound,' says historian Sir Robert Wall, 'One would think that they wouldn't make the same mistake again, and that's a source of great puzzlement to me. How that happened, goodness knows, but it did, and they got away with it.'

The *Canberra* was ordered to leave San Carlos Bay, and sailed at 11pm on that night for South Georgia, where the *QE2* lay in comparative safety, to collect the reinforcing 5th Brigade, which she brought back to San Carlos, this time in fog which made further air attacks impossible. In spite of the danger, Dennis Scott-Masson remembers it all as being 'a very marvellous experience'. And his ship had proved herself made of the right stuff:

> Our affection for the 'Great White Whale' became very strong indeed. Still is. She did remarkably well. We'd come back from a three-month round-the-world voyage, and set off within three days for another three-month deployment to the Falklands and Ascension Island, and she never, ever, once let us down. She never faltered. The engine sang like a sewing machine. We

refuelled at sea, which was a unique experience for us, from Royal Fleet Auxiliary tankers, thousands of tons of oil. And the ship was absolutely marvellous.

The Falklands conflict was bloody. Many men on both sides died or were hideously wounded in what seemed to some commentators at the time to be a throwback to the colonial era, a long-outdated way of settling disagreements. Later, the Gulf War might perhaps cast doubt on this point of view, but national pride is unpredictable, and nations will do much to protect their interests, however irrational it may seem afterwards. Throwback or not, the campaign was a demonstration of the strength of British arms and the determination of British seamen and women. And in a way it sounded the last post, not only for an empire, but for the great ships that once held it together.

P&O have announced that the *Canberra* is going out of service, to a fate unknown. For her old captain, Dennis Scott-Masson, it is a sad moment:

> She looks as good as the say she came out of Harland & Wolff's in 1961, probably better. But modern regulations dictate that it's too expensive to upgrade her from a safety point of view. A ship is as mortal as we are, and she has to come to the end of her life. And she's had a very illustrious life. She's a very old ship by ship standards. She'll be thirty-six years old when she retires, which by any yardstick is a very good innings. Personally I would like to see her scrapped. That's the proper end for a ship.

In 1982, after the Argentine surrender, *Canberra* repatriated thousands of Argentine prisoners-of-war to South America, and returned to Southampton and an old-fashioned welcome that Dennis Scott-Masson is happier to recall:

> It happened to be a perfect summer's day, a slight mist over Southampton water as we approached. My wife, who was obviously on the quayside, said it was quite moving to see the ship coming out of the mist. And all these thousands of people lining the quay, lining the shore all the way down Southampton Water, and of course all the yachts that were around, hundreds and hundreds of them. Yes, it was a very emotional time, and a very happy time.

. . . Long Live The Queen

On the banks of the Clyde, at the John Brown shipbuilding works outside Glasgow, you can still see the long, thin strip of highly compressed land on which some of the greatest liners in history were built. There are no monuments, plaques or reminders of any sort that it was here that the *Lusitania, Aquitania, Queen Mary, Queen Elizabeth,* the *QE2*, and scores of other great passenger ships were conceived and created by the genius of the Clydebank shipbuilders. It's a sad and deserted patch of land, directly opposite the River Cart, the tributary of the Clyde that gave this site the additional girth of water that 'superliners' require on launching day.

The old buildings in which the plates were cut and rolled and the largest and most powerful marine engines in the world were designed and built are also still there, looking from the outside much the same as they have since the turn of the century. The temporary ceremonial launching platforms on which British monarchs, their consorts and families stood to launch the giant Cunarders are, of course, long gone, but for the people of the Clydebank, the memories remain.

Across the Irish Sea, in Harland & Wolff's Belfast yards, it

The old section of Harland & Wolff's shipbuilding yard in Belfast, as it looks today.

The immortal 80,750-ton *Queen Mary*, arguably the most famous liner ever built, today preserved as a floating hotel, tourist attraction and maritime museum at Long Beach, California.

is much the same today, except that in the huge shipbuilding complex they still build giant freighters and tankers. But in one corner of a deserted car park, the two concrete ramps on which the *Olympic* and *Titanic* were built remain untouched, stark reminders of the great White Star liners this yard produced. And overlooking this same car park, the high-ceilinged drawing-rooms, and the administration offices where the *Olympic* plans were drawn and later modified for her sister ship *Titanic*, are deserted

and in a state of disrepair. One day, perhaps, they will be restored to house the great wealth of historic material that records the era when the men of Belfast built many of the world's greatest passenger liners.

In Bristol, you can go on board the lovingly restored *Great Britain* – and gaze in wonder at the genius of Brunel's creation, the world's first ocean liner. And in Liverpool, the docks where passengers and immigrants boarded liners bound for the New World for almost a century are now

LEFT:
A frozen moment in history: the bow rail of the *Titanic* appears through the watery darkness that cloaks the amazingly preserved wreck of the famous White Star liner on the bottom of the North Atlantic Ocean.

deserted but Cunard's old head-office building still overlooks the scene of so many historic departures and arrivals. Even the docks at Southampton, and the huge King George V dry dock, built to take the giant Cunard *Queen*s, the famous passenger terminal building and the old railway platforms where the boat trains from London added to the hustle and bustle of sailing and arrival days for the liners, lie practically deserted, or have gone altogether.

So spread throughout this once great maritime nation are poignant reminders of the era when Britain ruled the waves, and ocean liners were playing a significant role in changing the world we live in. Tangible reminders of the greatness of those mighty ships are few and far between, particularly as those who sailed on them are beginning to disappear for ever. In Long Beach, California, the mighty *Queen Mary* is a lone relic, not preserved as many would wish, but nevertheless there for the world to enjoy and marvel at.

Dr Robert Ballard, the discoverer of the *Titanic* and a man who has dedicated a large part of his professional life searching for and exploring wrecks, points out that the one remaining preserve of many of the greatest liners ever built is on the floor of the oceans. Perhaps, one day, like Jules Verne's

LEFT:
'In the world of cruising there's a lot of plain vanilla, there's occasionally French vanilla, but we want to be Tutti Fruitti and Rocky Road. We want to have a lot of pizzazz and excitement.'
– Bob Dickinson, President, Carnival Cruise Lines. And that's exactly what a Carnival ship provides!

151

fiction hero, Captain Nemo, we will all be able to enter giant submarines to explore these depths and visit the *Titanic, Lusitania, Britannic, Andrea Doria* and a host of other famous ships, many remarkably preserved in a time warp, waiting to be discovered.

It was giant passenger liners that became the proud symbols of the British Empire's strength and mirrored its technological achievements for the world to see in awe and envy. But that era passed as the dominions of empire gained their independence, and rival industrial nations caught up with and moved out of the shadow and influence of British dominance of industry and state.

These factors coincided with the introduction of the jet airliner and the revolution in intercontinental travel that came as the skies took over from the sea lanes of the world. With profit pulled from under the feet of the liner companies, the yards that built their ships for almost a century were dealt a mortal blow. Professor Slaven:

> If British shipowners were no longer ordering liners there was no demand for them. It didn't take very long before they lost the capability to build them. And with a twenty-year gap between the traditional liner market and the emergence of the new cruise-liner market, by the time that came on stream, the British shipyards had changed their product mix, their skills, their expertise and direction, which made it really quite impossible for them to get back into the new liner market in any meaningful way.

As the international cruise-line business emerged as an industry that would soon see more people travelling on the oceans of the world than ever before, a small number of yards outside Britain realized the potential in building ships for this new market. The major yards were based in Finland, Germany, France and Italy all of which, as Professor Slaven comments:

> . . . got into it with the help of government subsidies . . . they came into the market and made a real success of it. Today there's twenty-two new cruise-liners on order in world shipyards, most of them in European yards, but not in Britain. The British simply no longer have the expertise to do it.

With the largest percentage of world cruising happening in the tropical waters of the Caribbean, there is little wonder that this new leisure- and vacation-based industry is centred around the Florida ports of Miami, Fort Lauderdale, and Tampa. Like New York, the former bustling ports of the UK and Europe are now almost deserted by passenger liners and only see the new breed of cruise-liners on rare occasions when they are included as short stop-overs in their cruising itinerary. So the world of ocean liners has changed dramatically, from a British- and European-based transport industry offering a distinctive three-class service, to a multi-billion-dollar holiday and leisure industry largely operating in the tropical waters of the Caribbean in one-class ships.

Like all radical changes, there is criticism by some and slow acceptance by others. Dr John Brown, the man who worked on the design of the *Queen Mary* and *Queen Elizabeth*, and later became Managing Director of John Brown's on Clydebank, recalls an answer given by the captain of the *QE2* when asked by a passenger what he thought about modern cruise ships. 'Well, if you're talking of those ships down in the Caribbean, well, they're the ugliest thing you ever saw – like an American condominium.' John goes on to add his own opinion:

> I agree with him. Some of them are of passable appearance outside, but they're like a block of flats, and internally, I think the accommodation is much the same. It's like an egg-box of cabins, particularly the group in the Caribbean, mostly run by the Scandinavian lines, but some of the British too. They're run as five-night or seven-night cruises out of Miami or the east coast, and are nothing more than boozing expeditions.

Joe Farcas, the designer responsible for all of Carnival's cruise-liners, including the 100,000-ton *Destiny*, understandably has very different views:

> There is a nostalgic beauty about the old ships, but things have changed, and those things in a way are dinosaurs because if you did it again you would have a ship that would have to charge so much money that nobody could afford to go on them and the company would go out of business. You'd have a relic. The ships today have a beauty of their own. I think there are beautiful

ships being built today, they're different, that's all. They're not the *Normandie*, but they're beautiful in their own right.

Joe goes on to add: 'After all, ships have always been and still are, a business venture. They have to make money . . . the science and art of building ships [today], has allowed them to be built for a cost that can be transferred to an affordable passage price.'

Former captain of P&O's *Canberra*, Dennis Scott-Masson, the man in charge of 'the Big White Whale' during the Falklands War, doesn't think much of modern cruise-liners. 'I think the *Oriana* looks like a proper ship, and I have been on board and she is beautifully fitted out inside. But some of these new cruise-liners look like a floating block of flats. They don't appeal to me at all. Very modern inside, but that's taste.'

So the argument goes on, between traditional liner enthusiasts and practical realists who see the cruise-liner as an ever-evolving form of ocean-going vessel designed to meet the specific needs of today's passengers. The fact that there are more people making sea voyages today than ever before in the history of ocean liners surely says a lot for these modern liners. When asked what he felt was the difference between the cruise-ships of today and the great liners of yesterday, the maritime historian, author and philosopher of the sea, Frank Braynard, replied:

> Practically nothing. I love them all. They're just as good as the old ones. You don't have three classes. Maybe you have a little less elegance, but I don't think that really is true. Why, hell's bells, I've been on all these big ones – the *Sovereign of the Seas* and her sister ships, 75,000 tons each. Wonderful ships. I don't take the attitude at all that things have gone down because of cruising. Instead of that, you have a tremendous new public being educated to love going on ships.

Where many critics have doubts that Knut Kloster's dream ships, the gigantic *America World City* will ever be built, Frank has great hopes that it will, adding, 'We may see that now is just the beginning of the great liner, instead of the end of the great liner period.'

If Frank Braynard's hopes are realized, the world's first 100,000-ton liner, *Destiny*, has heralded a new and exciting era of ocean travel, an era surely as unpredictable as it was when designers and engineers like Isambard Kingdom Brunel, Robert Napier and Robert Fulton were producing radical, newfangled steamships a century and a half ago. It is impossible to imagine what the early shipping entrepreneurs, icons of the passenger-line business such as Samuel Cunard, Albert Ballin, Brodie Willcox and Arthur Anderson would think of today's giant cruise-liners and the vessels still on the drawing boards, like the *American America World City*. The size, shape and capabilities of today's ships would be hard for them to comprehend, but there is little doubt they would all doff their hats in salute to their modern-day counterparts: Ted and Micky Arison, Knut Kloster, Edward Stephan, founder of the Royal Caribbean Cruise Lines, the Italian Costa family, and every other shipping owner, big and small, who has contributed to the growth and success of the modern cruise-line industry.

In the twenty-year period, 1976 to 1996, an estimated 40 million passengers took a deep-water cruise. By the year 2000, present growth figures indicate a yearly total of 8 million passengers will make a cruise. The age of the great passenger liners may well be over, but the era of the super cruise-liners is only just beginning.

NOTES

1 Lacey, *op cit.*, page 124; D. Hutchings, *Queen Elizabeth, from Victory to Valhalla*, Kingfisher, 1990, page 105–6.

2 Boyd Cable, *A Hundred Year History of the P&O*, Ivor Nicholson & Watson Ltd., 1937, page 95.

3 *Selling the Sea*, pages 23–24.

4 *The Sunday Times* Insight Team, *The Falklands War*, Sphere, 1982, page 184.

5 *Ibid.*, page 185.

EVOLUTION OF SHAPE AND SIZE

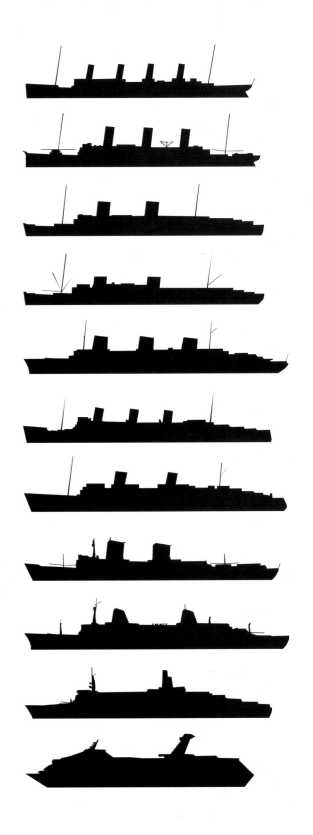

1819
SAVANNAH
Length: 110ft (34m)
320 tons

1837
SIRIUS
Length: 208ft (63m)
700 tons

1837
GREAT WESTERN
Length: 236ft (72m)
1,340 tons

1840
BRITTANIA
Length: 228ft (70m)
2,050 tons

1843
GREAT BRITAIN
Length: 289ft (88m)
3,500 tons

1858
GREAT EASTERN
Length: 689ft (210m)
18,915 tons

1888
CITY OF NEW YORK
Length: 560ft (171m)
10,500 tons

1897
KAISER WILHELM
DER GROSSE
Length: 655ft (200m)
14,349 tons

1899
OCEANIC
Length: 685ft (209m)
17,272 tons

1900
DEUTSCHLAND
Length: 684ft (208m)
16,500 tons

1907
LUSITANIA
Length: 790ft (241m)
32,000 tons

1912
TITANIC
Length: 883ft (269m)
46,500 tons

1913
IMPERATOR
Length: 909ft (277m)
52,200 tons

1929
BREMEN
Length: 938ft (286m)
51,650 tons

1930
EUROPA
Length: 941ft (287m)
49,750 tons

1935
NORMANDIE
Length: 1,030ft (314m)
83,400 tons

1936
QUEEN MARY
Length: 975ft (297m)
80,750 tons

1940
QUEEN ELIZABETH
Length: 1029ft (314m)
83,650 tons

1952
UNITED STATES
Length: 990ft (302m)
53,500 tons

1961
FRANCE
Length: 1035ft (315m)
66,000 tons

1968
QUEEN ELIABETH II
Length: 963ft (294m)
65,850 tons

1996
DESTINY
Length: 893ft (272m)
101,000 tons

The propeller – since its introduction well over a century ago, a key element in the insatiable quest by ship designers and engineers for power, speed, economy and a vibration-free performance in the vessels they build. One of the *Oriana's* 2 x 32-ton variable pitch, four-bladed propellers: a gentle giant, measuring 5.8 metres in diameter, made and fitted with watch-like precision – a perfectly balanced masterpiece of engineering. Computers control the pitch of these monster screws, ensuring maximum performance for minimum engine power at speeds of 24 knots and more.

INDEX

Picture Acknowledgements

AKG, London: 91, 93;

Andy Newman/Carnival Cruise Lines: 139, 141, 151 bottom;

Associated Press: 95;

Australian War Memorial: 56, 58 top, 98 bottom, 98 top, 100;

Bill Miller Collection: 41, 42, 43 left, 43 right, 61, 62, 65, 68, 72 right, 75, 76, 77, 79, 80-81, 85, 86, 87, 90, 94, 101, 102, 106, 108, 113, 115, 117, 120, 123, 126, 133, 135, 136, 138;

Brunel University Library: 28-29, 30;

Campbell McAuley: 13;

Canal+Image: 50 bottom;

Corbis-Bettman/UPI: 16, 21, 44, 53 left, 128, 129;

Cunard Archives: 23;

Frank O. Braynard Collection: 59;

Glasgow University Archives: 45, 53 right, 82, 97;

Hamburg-South America Line: 107;

Hapag-Lloyd AG: 37; 52, 64, 67, 73, 74;

Harland & Wolff Collection, Ulster Folk Transport Museum: 47, 48;

Mary Evans Picture Library: 54;

National Maritime Museum: 27;

P&O Collection: 6, 10, 18, 19 bottom, 19 top, 25, 34, 35, 58 bottom, 71, 72 left, 122, 131, 142, 145 bottom, 145 top, 146, 155;

Peter Butt: 50 top, 51, 55, 63, 124, 149;

Rob McAuley: 57, 150;

Roger Scozzafava: 92;

Science Museum/Science & Society Picture Library: 22;

Sygma: 151 top;

The Walt Disney Company: 143 bottom left, 143 top;

Topham: 88, 109, 112, 121;

United States Line: 116;

World City Corporation: 143 bottom right

*'Evolution of Shape and Size' diagram: p15: © Artwork-Tad Designs Pty Limited/
The Liners Pty Limited*